MW01119820

Language, Media and Society

Language, Media and Society
Essence of Advertising Communication

Gajendra Singh Chauhan

Rawat Publications
Jaipur • New Delhi • Bangalore • Mumbai • Hyderabad • Guwahati

ISBN 81-316-0310-5
© Author, 2010

The publication of this book was financially supported by ICSSR and the responsibility for the facts stated, opinions expressed, or conclusions reached, is entirely that of the author and that ICSSR accepts no responsibility for them.

ICSSR Consultant: Professor R.S. Gautam

Published by
Prem Rawat for **Rawat Publications**
Satyam Apts, Sector 3, Jawahar Nagar, Jaipur 302 004 (India)
Phone: 0141 265 1748 / 7006 Fax: 0141 265 1748
E-mail: info@rawatbooks.com
Website: www.rawatbooks.com

New Delhi Office
4858/24, Ansari Road, Daryaganj, New Delhi 110 002
Phone: 011 2326 3290

Also at Bangalore, Mumbai, Hyderabad and Guwahati

Typeset by Rawat Computers, Jaipur
Printed at Nice Printing Press, New Delhi

For my Parents

God can't be everywhere—
that is why he made Mummy & Papa

Contents

Preface

Language is an indispensable component of the world, and enables us to think about our society and culture and interpret them. For these reasons, language is a quintessentially human activity that defines us as a species. The impulse to communicate is one of the most fundamental and basic human needs. Thus, communication is a central fact of human existence and social process.

The present work is based on an interdisciplinary study of language and advertising. The media and communication explosion in the last two decades have changed the life of modern man and the society in which he lives. This study seeks to examine the various important aspects of language as a means of communication through advertisements. The sole aim of the book is to study and interpret advertisements from various linguistic perspectives. It is an expedition into various ways of looking at advertisements and how they influence language and its users or consumers. The book draws explicit attention to everyday language and its representation in advertisements. Although the main thrust is on language, it is not concerned with language alone. It also examines the context of communication, who is communicating with whom and why, in what kind of society, and through what medium. The business objectives, social relevance and aesthetic value of advertising are discussed and analysed comprehensively across a wide range of media, from traditional media to the Internet, from billboards to SMS.

The introduction looks at language, society and culture as an important link and addresses their interdependent existence. Chapter 1 presents language as an important means of communication and highlights how advertising communication becomes effective and saleable with language. Chapter 2 offers a broad view of the world of advertising and investigates the objectives, ideologies and techniques of advertising communication.

Chapter 3 delves into the sociolinguistic setting of Arunachal Pradesh and shows the ways in which the local tribal people communicate with each other in the absence of a regional language and a standard script for writing. This chapter also includes code mixing, a popular trend in advertising communication, and demystifies the sexist language of advertisements. Chapter 4 examines the persuasive effects of language on our everyday opinions, perceptions and attitudes.

Chapter 5 analyses select advertising discourses and evaluates them, using the yardstick of the cooperative principle. Chapter 6 seeks to find how visual messages are formed and given meaning through the semiotic analysis of advertisements. The practitioners of the semiotic school believe that the meanings of pictures are not in the pictures, but in what we bring to them. Chapter 7 focuses on the profound impact of the Internet on the English language and the ways in which we communicate.

Chapter 8 features a comparative study of Hindi and English advertising practices and the manner in which they differ. It also looks at how Hindi suddenly became a hot and happening medium for advertisements. In concluding Chapter 9, having come full circle, I reinvent the major issues that have niggled at me over the years.

I hope that younger entrants in the discipline of applied linguistics and advertising media will find something of interest and merit in this book. It should be useful for both students and teachers, working not only in the language and literature department, but also in the rapidly developing areas of cultural and media studies.

Acknowledgement

No book is ever really the product of a solitary scholar. While pursuing my research work, I came across many people who helped to make this work possible.

I undertook this interdisciplinary study under the scholarly guidance of Prof B.Y. Lalithamba, who introduced me to the fascinating world of advertising communication. She is an enlightened linguist, a workaholic and an extremely simple human being. She went through almost every word in my manuscript and pushed me to think differently. I thank her for being decent, supportive and, not least, for the wonderful South Indian dishes she fed me. Further, I would like to thank Dr M.S. Parmar, who helped me in balancing my work with his professional acumen and profound knowledge of modern ways of mass communication.

This research might have been different if the Indian Council of Social Science Research (ICSSR), New Delhi had not offered me a study grant to visit institutes and libraries in order to collect material. To ICSSR goes a big thank you for believing in my work and awarding the publication grant. I extend my thanks also to the librarians of the National Social Science Documentation Centre (NASSDOC), New Delhi, Jawaharlal Nehru University (JNU),

New Delhi, and Central Institute of English and Foreign Languages (CIEFL), Shillong, for their cooperation and technical assistance.

Other scholars who have had an immeasurable influence on my work include Binod Mishra, M.S. Sharma, D.P. Panda, Harish Sharma, S.N. Jha, K.K. Mishra, P.K. Bhawsar, Shoib Adil and Suman Kumar. To all of them, I owe a massive debt. They have been sources of immense moral support and encouragement to me.

Words fail to express my gratitude to my beloved wife, Yogeeta Chouhan, who stayed away from me during the entire period while I was working on this project. She looked after our children, Khush and Vivy, and never let them feel my absence.

I owe my gratitude also to my loving parents, brother and sister-in-law, who always stood by me in times of stress and supported me whenever I needed them most.

There are many advertisements reproduced and quoted in this book. I am thankful to all the corporate houses and media groups for allowing me to use their brand names in this book.

My thanks are due to Mr Pranit Rawat of Rawat Publications, Jaipur, who has been extremely sensible and cooperative in the entire process of publication of this book.

Gajendra Singh Chauhan

Introduction

Language, Society and Culture

The genesis of language is not to be sought in the prosaic, but in the poetic side of life; the source of speech is not gloomy seriousness, but merry play and youthful hilarity ... . In primitive speech I hear the laughing cries of exultation when lads and lassies vied with one another to attract the attention of the other sex, when everybody sang his merriest and danced his bravest to lure a pair of eyes to throw admiring glances in his direction. Language was born in the courting days of mankind.

— Otto Jespersen (1921)

Language, Society and Culture

The purpose of the present research was quite explicit in my mind and, from the beginning, I realised that a work of this nature would be extensive, interesting and, of course, demanding. The multidimensional role of language in any society is beyond comparison. Language is the identity of an individual, of a community and of a nation. We can easily sense the warmth of its existence and the 'pervasiveness' of its application in our everyday life. And it is this vividness of language that lured me to explore its magical power in the world of advertising. Before I discuss specific areas of research, I would like to underline the inspiring bond between language, society and culture.

No society exists without language. Language and society are intimately tied to each other. Language is an institution designed, modified and extended (some purists might even say distorted) to meet the ever-changing needs of society and culture. Human beings need a vehicle to communicate their needs, likings, choices and desires, and language makes communication possible in every situation. If society and culture are the heart and soul of the human being, language is the body. Simeon Potter rightly remarks, "Language stands in its right place in the Dewey decimal classification system between sociology and natural science because it is a social activity on the one hand and a scientific system on the other. It was an outstanding achievement of nineteenth century philologists that they succeeded in establishing the autonomy of their science as an independent discipline in its own right".[1]

Language is the product of a culture. Since time immemorial, language has been the chief transmitter of cultural and social values. Unless there is meaningful cultural contact among people, no effective communication can take place. In one area of South America, missionaries have been working for more than three decades, but none of them has learned to speak the Indian language with any degree of intelligibility. The result is that there are not more than sixteen Indians who are said to be 'converted' and more than half of these are regarded as having 'back slidden'. The reason is quite simple: If culture cannot transmit its own concepts except by language, how can missionaries expect to disseminate wholly foreign concepts without using the only language which the people really understand?

If languages are a part and a mechanism of culture, they are also, in a sense, a model of culture. The use of honorific language by and about the respective classes of a culture so closely reflects the social structure that we can describe the linguistic usage as a kind of model of what happens in the society. If, as in England, one's accent betrays one's social class and certain positions in business or society are restricted to those who possess the culturally acceptable accent, language becomes, in a sense, a model of this social classification.

Language is an important part of human behaviour, governed by tradition and culture. The family is the fundamental unit in human society and a child's acquisition of language depends largely upon the quality of the family life of which it forms a part. Good breeding and upbringing may contribute more to the child's linguistic development than formal education. A boy or girl who hears lively conversation and discussion among people of all ages within the family circle over a long period of years enjoys untold advantages.

However, language, like all parts of culture, is an essentially arbitrary system. This 'arbitrariness' includes not only sounds and corresponding meanings, but also grammatical structure. If we wish to emphasise something, we may repeat it, as, for example, very, very good. But in Hiligaynon, spoken in the central Philippines, the repetition of an expression makes it less strong than if it were said once. Every society has its own way of describing experiences, but we assume that they should employ our idiom. Eugene A. Nida puts it brilliantly when he says that we talk about the 'eye of a needle', but the Eastern Otomi in Mexico insist that it should be 'the ear of a needle', the Kekchi Indians of Guatemala call it the 'face of the needle' and still other people call it the 'nostril of the needle', 'hole of the needle' or even 'foot of the needle'.[2]

There is a sharp deviation of meaning in language from one cultural group to another. Sometimes, we find absolute control in the expression of the same phrase or idiom. This versatility of language compels us to comprehend a people's culture and society first before establishing an effective communication bond with them. We take 'a big heart' to mean generosity, but the Huaves of Southern Mexico say that it means 'bravery', while the Tzeltals, also living in Southern Mexico, interpret it as 'forgiving'.

However, the Shilluks of Anglo-Egyptian Sudan say that a person with 'a big heart' is stingy, while someone with 'a small heart' is generous. They explain the idiom in cultural terms by saying that a stingy, selfish man has accumulated all that he can and put it all away in his heart, which is why it is a big heart. On the other hand, the generous man has given away almost all his possessions, so his heart is small. The Akhas of Burma use the phrase, 'a big heart', to describe a conceited man, while one who has 'a small heart' is cowardly. Such irregularities illustrate the arbitrary character of language, but they do not invalidate the fact that despite all such discrepancies, there is a structure to language, even as there is a structure to culture.

It is easy enough to understand that languages must undergo changes in their vocabularies because of cultural modifications and word borrowing from the outside world. But we seldom realise how extensive these vocabulary changes can be. Though English is basically a Germanic language, it has a vocabulary which is more than half derived from non-Germanic sources. The English language has borrowed thousands of words from all over the world—'cuisine' and 'blonde' from French, 'arcade' and 'carpet' from Italian, 'barbecue' and 'cafetaria' from Spanish, 'bonus' and 'alien' from Latin, 'phenomenon' and 'crisis' from Greek, 'coca' and 'jerky' from Quechua, and so on.

"All living languages are constantly changing. 'God be with you', the greeting of an earlier century, became the 'Goodbye' of today, while today's 'Let's go eat' is rapidly becoming tomorrow's 'Skweet'. One only needs to read the first few lines of Chaucer's *Canterbury Tales* to realise how much English has changed since the fourteenth century:

> Whan that Aprille with his shoures soote
> The droughte of Marche both perced to the roote
> And bathed every veyne in swich licour,
> Of which vertu engendred is the flour.

We can recognise many of the words, because of the archaic character of contemporary English spelling, but if we heard these lines recited by a Middle English poet, we would probably not recognise a single word or phrase".[3]

The meanings of words reflect culture. The dependence of meaning upon cultural contexts is perfectly obvious when children are in the process of learning a language. The little girl who defined 'amen' as meaning 'Now you can open your eyes' understood unconsciously the relationship between language and its cultural context. "The connotations of words abound in cultural influences. When a person is denied a visa to enter a country as a 'missionary', but is granted entrance later when he applies as a 'pastor' or a 'preacher of the gospel', it is perfectly obvious that the real trouble lies in the cultural associations of the word 'missionary', implying, as it does, to most people, an irksome superiority-inferiority relationship. There is nothing intrinsically wrong with the word, but it cannot be isolated from the cultural environment of which it is an inseparable part".[4]

By putting words together, one cannot draw the meaning of a phrase. The meaning of 'cooling one's heels' cannot be understood by adding up the meanings of the individual words. The meaning of this phrase is more than the sum total of the expression. Phrases in any language are understood mostly by the simple process of adding together the meanings of the component parts, which is why people fail to understand idioms and phrases. Consider another example, taken from a newspaper advertisement, and think not only about what the words might mean, but also about what the advertiser intended them to mean:

Fall Baby Sale

In the normal context of our present society, we assume that this store has not gone into the business of selling young children over the counter, but rather, that its advertising clothes for babies. The word, 'clothes', does not appear anywhere in the advertisement. But our normal interpretation would be that the advertiser intended us to understand his message as relating to the sale of baby clothes and not, we trust, of babies.[5]

True translation reproduces the closest natural equivalent, first in meaning and second in style. Translation is not merely conveying information, but expressing in an equivalent style something of the emotionally charged character of the original. Linguistic parallels are even more striking because they reveal subtle underlying differences. In English, we may be told 'to mind our own business', but an Uduk in the Sudan tells his bothersome neighbour, "Go sit in your own shade!" We can describe an obnoxious person as 'a pain in the neck', while the Marshallese will talk about the same kind of pest as 'a fishbone in one's throat'. Our phrase, 'butterflies in the stomach', is not very different from the way the Choutals of Oaxaca, Mexico, describe nervous worry: 'butterflies in the heart'.

India has often been characterised as a 'cultural continent'—a land with many different traditions and faiths, institutionalised or otherwise, many diverse languages, both literary and non-literary, and writing systems derived from Brahmi, Semitic, Roman and other traditions.

The significance of language as a cultural dynamic and national symbol is fully evident in the attempt of the father of our nation, Mahatma Gandhi. He realised the imperative of culture-bound concepts when communicating with the Indian masses and brought into currency terms from Indian reality, such as 'swadeshi', 'satyagraha', 'ahimsa', 'Harijan' and 'Ram Rajya'. "Such cross-cultural distortions become more apparent in a scientific discourse, as, for example, when 'dharma' is narrowly interpreted as 'religion' and 'jati', 'varna' and *'gotra'* as 'caste'. Similarly, the concept, 'secularism', is beyond the reach of an average Indian mind and its translations in Indian languages are not very satisfactory. The Sanskrit coinage, *'dharmnirpekshta'* ('religious neutrality') appears to be a hollow term; a metaphor like *Vasudhaiva kutumbakam* (All the universe is a family) would be better understood in the context of Indian reality."[6]

The selection of a research topic is in many ways a difficult task. The topic of my study, 'Linguistics of Advertisements: Communication through English and Other Indian Languages', was selected after thoughtful consideration of many linguistic aspects. In fact, it was a wonderful subject for me because I was inclined to work on an interdisciplinary area featuring language and mass communication. The language used in advertisements is witty, charming and sometimes mysterious. Its basic objective is to convert an indifferent customer into a potential buyer. Language does the job of icing on the cake of advertisement. It is like a cherry on an ice cream. The copywriter is the man who, with this powerful tool, writes a new history of extraordinary sales and profit. Copywriters are always in search of smarter ways to get customers to part with their money.

One more reason why I was tempted to choose this topic is that not much work has been done in this area. Although some works have touched upon similar themes, the present work is novel in its approach and in the aspects it studies. The present research endeavours to investigate the salient linguistic features of each advertisement and to identify variations in the way they are used. It talks in precise terms about the strategies that advertisers employ and the linguistic attitudes they hold and enables the reader to understand their beliefs and concerns about language.

The research design of the present work is analytical and literary in nature and an interdisciplinary aspect is the key feature of the investigation. Keeping in view the objectives of the work, the whole study was planned to investigate the subtleties of the language of advertising in the Indian context on the yardsticks of the cultural, sociopsychological and semiotic components of language.

Chapter 1 provides an overview of language and society and the role of language in modern advertising. Human society depends upon constantly operative communication. Deprived of communication, society would cease to exist. Chapter 2 takes up the essence of the advertising world with a focus on copywriting for various media. Chapter 3 is based on the sociolinguistic aspects of advertisements. Language is changing day by day in consonance with the changing needs of people. Advertisements are the best mirror of the social changes and trends that are coming into effect today and affecting the masses.

Chapter 4 features the psycholinguistic aspect of advertisements. The copywriter's criterion for creating an advertisement is the finest form of deep analysis and strong command over his customers and market. Language is the weapon that he uses on the human psyche. The copywriter knows the pulse of society and plans his advertisements accordingly to cast his spell over customers. It highlights the ways to execute creative strategy and some criteria for evaluating advertisements. Chapter 5 covers a discourse analysis of print advertisements. We are continually taking part in conversational interactions where a great deal of what is meant is not actually present in what is said. Chapter 6 explores the subtleties of visual images and seeks the meaning from visuals available in advertising messages. Chapter 7 provides an interesting discussion on the Internet, mobile phones and how companies are using them as a medium for communicating with customers. With the development of information technology, the whole world is at our doorstep and the concept of the global village is a reality.

Chapter 8 features a brief analysis of English and Hindi advertisements. Dialects, too, could be a means of communication in generating social consciousness among the masses in the absence of a standard language. The concluding chapter summarises all the findings of the previous chapters.

This research study has been carried out using the sampling method. It is a linguistic study of advertisements and the researcher has carefully chosen samples of ads from various sources of media, such as television, radio, newspapers, the Internet and display hoardings. Advertisements have been taken from the automobile, cosmetics, textiles, dairy, hotel, aviation, tourism and beverage sectors. The range is quite wide because the language of advertising varies with the products.

Notes

1. Potter, Simeon, 1975. *Language in the Modern World.* London: Audre Deutsch Ltd., p. 159.
2. Nida, Eugene A., 1954. *Customs and Cultures.* New York: Harper & Row, p. 206.
3. Ibid., p. 208.
4. Ibid., p. 211.
5. Yule, George, 1995. *The Study of Language.* Cambridge: Cambridge University Press, p. 98.
6. Khubchandani, Lachman M., 1991. *Language, Culture and Nation-Building.* New Delhi: Manohar Publications, p. 10.

One

Language and Advertising Communication

Doing business without advertising is like winking at a girl in the dark; you know what you are doing, but nobody else does.

— Steward H. Britt

It is probably true to say that of all ways in which language is used, advertising is the one that is most likely to arouse strong feelings. It is the one form of communication in which human beings are keenly and increasingly involved. In fact, advertising is multidimensional. It is a form of mass communication, a powerful marketing tool, a component of the economic system, a means of financing the mass media, a social institution, an art form, an instrument of business management, a field of employment and a profession.

Advertising is communication that involves all the linguistic aspects of language, which is the medium through which the main transmission of the message of an advertisement is carried out, though visual aids often help to amplify the message. Language manipulates and shapes communication to such an extent that the subtlest nuances of words are recorded in communication and the slightest shift in emphasis may affect considerable differences in meaning. Therefore, advertising, in which getting the message across is of prime importance, cannot afford to indulge in the uncritical use of language. The copywriter is compelled to exercise extremely careful judgement in the composition of an advertisement.

Advertising for the purposes of transmission of information dates back to ancient Greece and Rome. Criers and signs were used to disseminate information about goods and services well before the development of printing. Even during the Middle Ages, advertising signs were used extensively. These signs generally consisted of illustrations of symbols of the products advertised. The first upsurge in advertising came after the development of printing. When printing techniques were perfected and as the printing industry developed, the signs were replaced by written words or messages. Language became the major tool of copywriters in transmitting their messages to the people.

Language is a means of mass communication and, when it is used in the form of advertisements, it makes mass selling possible. A baby crying for its feed, a girl wooing Prince Charming, a housewife hankering for a new sari—all these are aspects of advertisements. They want to communicate, to persuade, to influence and to lead to some action. There is a semblance of advertising in the many activities of human beings, especially those activities which influence others, either favourably or otherwise. This form of communication is part of human life and it exists and grows with human society. We can witness in nature dancing daffodils or sweet-smelling roses, which silently invite butterflies to achieve the objective of pollination. Fruits, flora and fauna all advertised themselves even before man existed. Informally, advertising is interwoven with nature and the evolution of the world. Alyque Padamsee, well-known advertising and theatre personality and former managing director of Lintas, says, "When a man wears a trouser-shirt ensemble instead of a dhoti, he is advertising that he is Westernised. When a woman wears lipstick, she is advertising that she wants to look beautiful. When a neta (politician) delivers a speech, he is advertising that he wants to be noticed. Ads are parts of human nature to be noticed."

The effectiveness of communication depends upon to what extent the advertising message is received and accepted by the target audience. Several models have been developed, which have specifically identified the sequence of events that must take place between receipt of the message and the desired action.

One school of advertising claims that whole secret of successful advertising lies in the formula, AIDA, which stands for Attention, Interest, Desire and Action, which are the things that you have to generate, in this order, to win your audience.

Tony Harrison says, "In the formula itself, there is nothing particularly harmful since some series of gates must in truth be gone through if a sale is to be reached. People can hardly be persuaded to take the action of buying unless, first, some sort of wish to possess the product has been created. They can hardly feel that desire unless they have first been interested, and they can hardly be interested unless their attention has been gained. The problem with the formula is that, because it looks at the craft of ad-making as a series of steps, it often tends to produce ads that also reflect those steps. First, they shout 'Stop!' or 'Look!' at you, attempting to gain your attention. Then they bring in a headline which is supposed to arouse interest. This is followed by some copy directed towards the arousal of desire and the ad closes with a plea to 'Get some today'. Such advertisements do not achieve very much".[1]

Harrison further explains, "In fact, despite the distinction drawn by AIDA devotees, attracting attention and arousing interest are almost the same thing. At least, they form a logical continuum, since borrowed attention values (the bikini-clad girl in

the ad for spark plugs) are known not to work. And the key to this desirable effect is to discover the point where the product's advantages and the relevant self-interest of the reader overlap".[2]

Peter F. Drucker recounts the old riddle asked by the mystics of many religions, "Is there a sound in the forest if a tree crashes down and there is no one around to hear it?" The answer is no. True, the tree, while falling, sets up sound waves in the air, but it takes the human ear to convert those waves into a discernible noise. This is a simple, but humbling, riddle for would-be communicators to remember. *Communication takes place in the ear of the listener, not in the mouth of the speaker.*

So, since communication is at the heart of successful advertising, it is rarely sufficient simply to say what it is that our copy strategy wishes us to communicate. Simply saying it does not often result in it being truly communicated. We generate the required sound waves, but the ears that should hear are deaf.

The copywriter is a juggler. He knows which words will be most emotional and appealing in a headline and will attract customers. It is the power of language that sells a product like hot cakes and takes out money from the pockets of buyers. It is not necessary that the copywriter always be successful in communicating the right message. In some ads, he may fail to deliver the desired results because he is unable to establish an effective nexus between the producer and the consumer. Language, when not used artistically, fails to stir the minds of the people. But in certain advertisements, the vividness of language is at its brightest. Why is it that the nursery rhymes we learnt years ago still echo in our mind when so many other worthier and more important things have been forgotten? Some of the most effective advertising has this quality of sticking in the mind because of something incantatory and rhythmic in its words, because of something slightly odd and distinctive in its visual, because of a jingle that we cannot get out of our heads.

Language has to be precise and logical to make an immediate impact on the buyer. It has to be literary and artistic to arrest his attention. It has to be unpretentious and, at the same time, ingenious and efficient in delivering the message it carries. Advertisements have to speak the consumers' language and make sure that the concepts presented are acceptable. An example is the

Hero Honda motorcycle advertisement, which showed the product with an eager aficionado riding it, and just two words, *'Men's Lib'*. Or the ad that laid out neat rows of fruit-flavoured Lifesavers and the injunction, *'Please Do Not Lick This Page'*.

An award-winning ad for Nulon hand cream years ago showed a large picture of a woman's hands under water and the headline: *'Picture of a Lady Drying Her Hands'*. Handcare was not a new concept and Nulon did more or less what other hand lotions did. But the effect of presenting the apparent contradiction, that wetting your hands actually dried them, was a novel, involving suggestion. The people who read the ad recognised at once what it was saying. It fitted into their established pattern of things, but still had the benefit of some surprise and novelty.

Language leaves a lasting impression on the minds of the masses. Our involvement with language is deep and permanent and we are immeasurably affected by the written words in an advertisement. Most of us feel that advertising is a powerful persuasive tool for the marketer to create a demand for his product. Consumers usually feel that they have nothing to gain from an advertisement. Most of us do not have full faith in the correctness of an advertising message. We have a predetermined impression that advertisements are exaggerations, highlighting benefits of the product that are not too important, while concealing more important drawbacks. In short, we do not take any advertisement message seriously and have stereotypical reactions to almost all advertisements.

The copywriter is cautious in the selection of words and phrases while writing advertisement copy. He studies the temperament of the buyer and makes use of only that language that he is assured will evoke the desired reaction to what he wants to sell. Now, we will see how the application of different words for the same product can influence buyers. If we look in any newspaper, we will see notices like this one:

For Sale   For Sale

Small House   Very Desirable Residence

Here we have two words, both of which mean a place to live in, used about the same object. The first house agent calls it a small house in the ad, the second a desirable residence. Both house and residence are true symbols. But the word, 'residence', suggests riches, comfort and luxury. Although this house may be neither comfortable nor luxurious, so great is the magic of words that the very act of calling a small house a desirable residence has the power to make many people believe that it is indeed a desirable residence. In the advertisement, the very use of the word, 'residence', changes the reality of the actual fact.

Due to the tough competition among companies and overcrowding of products in the market, advertisers rely greatly on the language of their ads to attract buyers. Advertising agencies are in search of gifted writers who can beguile customers with the beauty of their language. The effective use of language has become the need of the hour to enhance sales and earn more profit. A dusky woman will buy an expensive tube of fairness cream because the advertisement assures her instant beauty, a great career and a perfect marriage if she uses it. Marketing strategist Charles Renson comments, "In our factories, we produce cosmetics, but in our drug stores, we sell hope." So, it is advertisements that make us think that when we buy a Maruti car, we buy prestige, and when we buy a bottle of Chyawanprash, we buy vigour and vitality. They sell their products and we buy our happiness, prosperity and status from them.

That rare moment your wife thinks you look better than Shahrukh

sangini
DIAMOND JEWELLERY

Why wait to tell her she's special.
Gift her a Sangini.

A DIAMOND IS FOREVER ◇ DTC

Culture is a basic part of human nature. It determines a person's wants and behaviour. Culture is learned. Children begin to be socialised right from the moment they come into the world. They acquire a basic set of values, perceptions, preferences and behaviour. This socialisation is conducted through the institutions of family, school, church and friends.

Advertising shapes our cultural values. But cultural values also shape our advertising. Advertising affects, not our core cultural values, but our subsidiary cultural values. For example, to get married is a core cultural value. Advertising cannot effectively change that by telling people not to marry. But to marry later, instead of at an early age, is a subsidiary cultural value. Advertising can definitely persuade people to marry late. Advertisements are a mirror of the society in which they operate. They reflect the cultural values of that society. ICICI Prudential stirred the market with its 'Sindoor' campaign in 2001 and its retirement solutions campaign, which carried the tagline, *'Retire from Work, Not Life'*. Instead of selling insurance by offering protection and safety, it used the appeal of self-respect and belongingness. Its 'Chintamani' ads also became an instant hit. Advertising improves our standard of living. It makes us realise how comfortable we can be with air-conditioners, computers, CDs, music systems, cars, washing machines, electric shavers and mobile phones. We buy these articles after advertising develops our interest in them. Thus, advertising creates new options in our lives.

no chinta, only money.

▪ **tax saving u/s 80 CCC**
▪ **regular pension for life**

sms SAVETAX to 7827*

Today, there is increasing give and take of culture. No matter how hard traditionalists try, there is no stopping the tidal wave of Western culture that is engulfing us. Adopting Chinese cuisine does not imply selling our souls to the Chinese civilisation. The give and take of culture, which advertising brings about in its contemporised form, is a symbol of universal togetherness. We have several cultural values as Indians. Indian advertising asks us to save for the marriage of our daughter or for the education of our

child. We are other-centred, not self-centred. And our advertisements reflect these cultural values of India. Thus, there are
advertisements for the well-being of the family, for the betterment
of a child, for a gift to a loved one, for the celebration of a festival,
and so on and so forth.

Most people have a love-hate relationship with advertising.
They love its gloss and sparkle, the imagery, the aspirations for a
better life, the self-indulgence, the feel-good factor, the way it
touches their senses and inner emotions. Yet, they hate it for its
power to influence them, for making them want more and spend
more, for making them buy things impulsively that they may
regret later, for its intrusion into their private space and favourite
pastimes. In totality, they see advertising as a necessary evil,
sometimes necessary, sometimes evil.[3]

Ethics is a choice between good and bad, between right and
wrong. Advertising, too, has ethical values. Advertising communication is a mix of art and facts subservient to ethical principles. In
order to be consumer-oriented, an advertisement will have to be
truthful and ethical. It should not mislead consumers, for, if that
happens, credibility is lost. Advertisement truths are to be viewed
from the consumer's point of view, and not in a narrow, legalistic
frame. However, it is very ticklish to judge this, for often, it is
difficult to establish a clear line of demarcation between what is
true and what is not. But advertisements as such are judged by
their impact and by their acceptance by consumers. What its ad
promises must be there in the performance of the product.

The language of advertisements should not be indecent and
obscene because advertising is a social process; it must honour
time-tested norms of social behaviour and should not ruffle our
sense of morality. Advertisers are blamed for creating desires
without showing the means to fulfil the desires.

Sometimes, women are projected as mere sex symbols in
advertisements. At other times, they are projected cheaply, with
their presence making little sense, as, for example, in the MRF

tyres advertisement. Well-known journalist Mrinal Pandey rightly remarks, "Advertising in India today mostly validates and glorifies a segregated world, where both visuals and copy highlight stereo-typical images of the women's world (family, illnesses, children, neighbours, cooking, sartorial jealousies, worries about husband's or mother-in-law's approval) and men's (boardroom victories, masculine rivalry) for the best-looking female, an obsession with speed and power and possessions, with woman as the ultimate one …. Therefore, it is no answer to women's daily debasement in our society, to show them in our advertisements as muscular superwomen who can and will excel in any field, and score off against men each time. What is actually required is a raising of the actual level of social consciousness in the country, about the basic human worth of a female child, girl, woman, and an honest appraisal and highlighting of her actual contribution in her various avatars as worker, mother, daughter, sister, grandmother, wife and companion ..."

Advertising plays a crucial part in the marketing approach by 'persuading' customers to 'buy' products and building a mutually beneficial relationship with them, thereby reducing the emphasis on having to 'sell'. Advertising is a constructive activity. It has a psychological impact on consumers and gives them greater satis-faction in using products.

The next chapter focuses on the craft of advertising. It lists all the ingredients that make ad copy complete and successful. People buy not a lipstick, but the concept of an outgoing, gorgeous, passionate woman. They do not buy a computer, but a solution to their complex problems. Thus, what the product really stands for is made known to us through advertising. Wills cigarettes stand for togetherness. Limca quenches thirst. Advertising affects our attitudes and values. It projects an image of ourselves to which we aspire.

Notes

1. Harrison, Tony, 1987. *A Handbook of Advertising Techniques.* London: Kogan Page Ltd., p. 118.
2. Ibid., p. 119.
3. Tiwari, Sanjay, 2003. *The (Un)common Sense of Advertising.* New Delhi: Response Books, p. 21.

Two

The World of Advertising

How to Hook a Customer

Innovation must make sense. Creativity must be relevant .... A well-worn anecdote has helped me gain a better grasp of what creativity may be about. Two blind beggars, we are told, were seated on different park benches. Each had an upturned hat beside him soliciting charity. One beggar had a placard on his breast, reading, "I am Blind." The other man's placard said, "It is Spring, and I am Blind." The latter's hat overflowed with money. History is silent about the other hat.

— Gerson Da Cunha

When a marketer or firm has developed a product to satisfy market demand after thoroughly analysing the market, there is need to establish contact with the target audience to eventually sell the product. Moreover, this has to be a mass contact, which means that the marketer needs to reach a large number of people so that his product may receive optimum exposure. Naturally, the best way to reach this mass market is through mass communication. Advertising is one such means of mass communication, along with publicity, sales promotion and public relations. As advertising is a means of mass communication, it makes mass selling possible. Being a vibrant force, advertising promotes the sale of goods, services, images and ideas through information and persuasion. But advertising by itself cannot sell a product. It cannot sell products that are of poor quality, products that are too expensive or products that do not come up to the expectations of the consumers. Advertising helps in selling through the art and business of persuasive communication. It is not a panacea that can transform a poor product or rejuvenate a declining market.

June A. Valladares defines advertising impressively. Herself an expert copywriter, Valladares speaks from her professional knowledge when she says, "Advertising is all about persuading people. It needs the skills of selling to be translated to the right medium, whether paper or celluloid. People tend to believe what they can see. The trick is to write that type of copy which brings your client's product to life before your customer's eyes, even if they are sitting in their own homes. In a shop, customers get a chance to see what they are buying. Notice how people behave in the supermarket or the bazaar. If the product is not packaged, they tend to handle the tomatoes, squeeze the fruit, they judge freshness and firmness, they smell the mangoes or papayas, they look and look and look and ask and feel before they decide to buy. This sort of behaviour annoys the shopkeeper, but customers are not daunted ... people want to see/touch/smell/taste the products they are buying. It is the copywriter's task to make them believe they are doing so—by reading your press ad, viewing your film or television commercial or hearing your radio spot".[1]

Basically, then, an advertisement is an announcement to the public of a product, service or idea through a medium to which the public has access. The medium may be print (such as newspapers, posters, banners and hoardings), electronic (radio, television, video, cable, mobile, Internet) or any other.

It was John E. Kennedy who defined copywriting as 'salesmanship in print'. Sidney Bernstein reinforces Kennedy's definition by describing 'advertising as a substitute for the human salesman'. Bernstein says, "Advertising is the most visible marketing tool which seeks to transmit an effective message from the marketer to a group of individuals. The marketer pays for sponsoring the advertising activity. Advertising, unlike salesmanship, which interacts with a buyer face to face, is non-personal. It is directed at a mass audience and not at an individual, as in personal selling".[2]

Advertising is a form of mass communication. In marketing communication, there is transmission of a message from the sender to the receiver. The end result of the communication process is the understanding of the message. Its effectiveness is determined by its success in accomplishing the following tasks:

- It must gain the attention of the receiver.
- It must be understood.
- It must stimulate the needs of the receiver and suggest appropriate methods to satisfy these needs.

Senders must be aware of the receivers or audiences they want to reach and the responses they want. They must be skilful in encoding the message, taking into account how the receiver or the audience is going to decode the message. Since the sender wants the receiver to understand the message, the sender must know as much as possible about the receiver before the message is designed. The communication sometimes fails to accomplish its purpose—creation of an appropriate response or understanding—when the message is distorted by noise elements. Noise includes poor message planning, busy audience members or careless feedback of response.

Advertising through the Ages

Advertising continues to be a dynamic profession that changes constantly. Advertising, as we understand it today, was not used until about 200 years ago. The use of advertising for the transmission of information dates back to ancient Greece and Rome.

Criers and signs were used to disseminate information about goods and services well before the development of printing. Even during the Middle Ages, advertising signs were used extensively. These signs consisted generally of illustrations of symbols of the products advertised. The first upsurge in advertising came after the development of printing. When printing techniques were perfected, and as this industry developed, the signs were replaced by written words and messages.

In the seventeenth century, when newspapers started appearing in various parts of the world, newspaper advertising began to develop. This was an important phase in the history of advertising. By the end of the century, a great number of commercial newspapers were published in England and elsewhere. The earliest ads in newspapers were for books, marriage offers, new beverages and travel. Soon advertising became the main source of revenue for newspapers and space selling came into existence. Around 1840, several people were selling space in newspapers in New York, Philadelphia and other metropolitan centres in countries where newspapers were published on a regular basis.

Still, most early newspaper advertisements were in the form of announcements. Those early advertisers were importers of products that were new to England. The first ad offering coffee appeared in a newspaper in England in 1652. Chocolate and tea were introduced through newspaper ads in 1657 and 1658, respectively, in England. This advertising was primarily 'pioneering advertising'. Competitive advertising came much later when ads attempted to convince readers about a product's superiority over other similar products. In the nineteenth century, advertising expanded in a huge way. Advertising agencies not only sold space in newspapers to clients, but also offered them several other services. Towards the end of the nineteenth century, creative advertisements were developed and printing came to be used in advertising.

Although the Americans were the forerunners of modern advertising, advertising had its roots in England. The Industrial

Revolution led to the expansion of mass-manufactured goods in Europe and America, making markets larger and larger. Localised markets were replaced by extended domestic national markets and international markets. This development altered the relationship between the makers and users of goods, and created a need for advertising.

Advertising has changed in some obvious ways. Electronic media, such as the Internet and wireless communication, are changing the media landscape and making advertising more intimate, interactive and personalised than was possible with traditional mass media.

The Genesis of Indian Advertising

The foundation of the professional Indian advertising business was laid by two English companies. In 1928, D.J. Keymer set up shop in Kolkata; a branch was opened later in Delhi. Over time, D.J. Keymer first became Bomas in Mumbai and later, Ogilvy Benson and Mather. In Kolkata, after D.J. Keymer closed office in the 1950s, the employees started Clarion Advertising Services Ltd as a cooperative.

In 1929, J. Walter Thompson of the US set up a branch in Mumbai in order to serve the General Motors business.

However, Indians had taken the initiative to set up advertising agencies even before these two well-known names. Dattaram Advertising was set up in 1905 by B. Dattaram, and continues to exist today as Dattaram Advertising Pvt. Ltd. Another early agency that continues to be in operation is the National Advertising Agency of Calcutta, which was set up in 1924 by Moni Lal Sen. Other early Indian agencies were Sista's in Mumbai and Tom and Bay in Pune.

Over the years, Indian advertising changed face several times. The pre-independence advertisements were mostly for ladies' goods, menswear, cotton goods, tailoring shops, teas, hotels, eating places, entertainment, travel and four-wheelers, all aimed at the Britishers, the Indian royalty and, in general, the upper strata of society in India. It is only after Independence and the abolition of the princely states that the newborn middle class received the attention of advertisers.

Advertising has played a vital role in the developmental process in India by creating a demand for consumer goods and raising the living standards of millions of people. Undoubtedly, Indian advertising has registered rapid growth and acquired a certain amount of professional character, but it is still to shed its elitist urban image and open up the country's vast rural market. Subhash Ghosal, a stalwart of Indian advertising, said, "Advertising is absolutely essential ... . But the trouble with Indian advertising is that it is not rooted in our ethos. It is Westernised, partly because most of our advertising is aimed at the urban consumer. But there should be a mix, so that advertising can sell products and yet retain the Indian flavour."

Different Types of Advertisements

Corporate

These include ads done for companies either through public service or good citizen campaigns or through their products, with the objective of creating an image. Corporate advertising is considered to be 'nice', rather than necessary. Coca-Cola's print ad talks about how its drinks bring 'little drops of joy' in your life.

Industrial

Industrial advertising does not sell only on emotions, like most consumer advertising does. It has to provide sound reasoning for buying the product in question. While drafting the copy, the demonstrative aspects must be emphasised. The price of the product is included as an important and essential element in industrial ad copy. It is meant for engineering and other industries and for original equipment manufacturers (OEMs).

Financial

These are advertisements for leasing and finance schemes, loan and deposit raising, certain types of bank advertising and for life and other forms of insurance.

Public Issue

These advertisements inform people about rights issues and announce the results of such issues.

Public Service

Campaigns sponsored by advertisers for causes such as HIV/AIDS, road safety and anti-pollution fall under the public

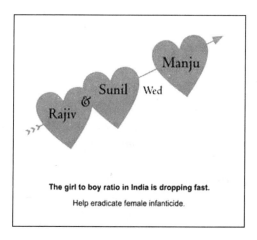

The girl to boy ratio in India is dropping fast.
Help eradicate female infanticide.

service category. Such advertisements seek to promote important social issues, and are created to promote greater awareness of such issues. The given ad is an eye opener and depicts brilliantly the poor ratio of males and females in India.

Classified

These are small advertisements, typically For Sale, Help Wanted, Matrimonial, To Let and Job Offer ads.

Consumer Perishables

These are ads that promote fast-moving consumer goods (FMCG), such as noodles, drinks, soaps and clothes.

Consumer Durables

These are ads for products, for which consumers have to pay a substantial sum, such as washing machines, television sets and cars.

Promotional

This is advertising meant for short-term sales, as, for example, to clear stocks through a contest, free offer or discount offer.

Teaser

These are a series of advertisements that may appear in the same newspaper on the same day or on consecutive days, which reveal the advertiser's message in stages.

Advertorial

This is advertising material presented in the form of an editorial message, as in *India Today* or *Reader's Digest*.

Direct Response

These include ads which require a direct response from the reader and usually have a coupon to be filled in at the end.

Buried Offers

Here, the advertiser buries an offer in the body copy—this is a gimmick used to test whether the advertisement is being noticed and read by the target audience.

Launch

This includes advertising that introduces a new product or an improved one.

Creativity in Advertising

Creativity in advertising is supposed to generate communicability, excitement and surprise from within the advertisement of a product. Creativity is where advertising lives; it is advertising's raison d'être. Creativity in advertising has two aspects of social import: first, the originality evident in the message communicated and in its presentation, and second, the improvements made in the life of the consumers or, as often stated, the effects on the consumers' standard of living.[3] Originality, ingenuity, inventiveness and imagination have been underlined as some of the basic abilities of creativity in the message communicated in an advertisement, which have changed observed perceptions. Many experts have defined the concept of creativity as a technique for producing ideas to achieve something new and relevant. James Young was of the view that the combination of existing in new and unexpected ways could be conceptualised as creativity.[4] Frank Barron highlighted this idea as "a discovery of something, i.e., not only novel but useful, is relevant or economical, elegant or valuable".[5]

The end result of being creative is ideas. Creative ideas are ideas which are new or relevant. Creative advertising ideas require some basic norms such as adaptability, durability, newness, oneness, relevance, memorability and simplicity. The creative process which generates the 'big idea' helps products to sell today and builds brands for the future. Air India's Maharaja, Raymond's

'Complete Man' and Bajaj Scooters' 'Hamara Bajaj' are some of the best-known examples of big ideas.

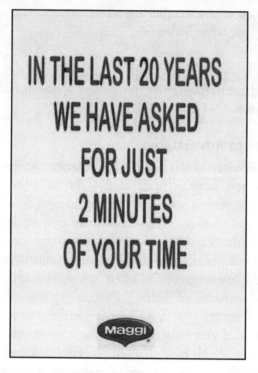

The Concept of Positioning

The positioning of a brand is the perception that it brings about in the minds of its target consumers. This perception reflects the essence of the brand in terms of its functional benefits in the consumers' judgement. It is relative to the consumers' perceptions of competing brands. The competing brands can be denoted as points or positions in the perceptual space of consumers and together make up a product class. "It is the sum of those attributes normally ascribed to it by consumers—its standing, its quality, the type of people who use it, its strengths, its weaknesses, any other unusual or memorable characteristics it may possess, its price and the value it represents."[6]

If we study advertisements, we will find that many companies and products are clearly positioned. Coca-Cola is ubiquitous, very American and clearly for teenagers. BMW is the chosen carriage of the affluent manager who has retained his youthfulness. Another excellent example of brand positioning is Maggi instant noodles. Positioning is a key word in modern-day advertising.

Unique Selling Proposition (USP)

The basic idea of creative advertising being unique for selling a product has been coined by different authorities in different ways. The phrase, unique selling proposition, or USP, as we know it better now, was coined by Rosser Reeves, in his famous book, *Reality in Advertising*. It became the catchword of the 1960s and the 1970s. With a USP, it is easy to create a distinct brand positioning in the minds of consumers.

A USP has three major features. First, each ad must make a proposition to the consumers. It must say to buyers what special benefit they are getting out of that product. For example, Dove soap offers the unique proposition that it is a quarter moisturising cream. Therefore, the benefit offered is that 'it won't dry your skin'.

Second, the proposition or promise made by the advertisement must be one that the competition has not made so far. There are very few genuine differences amongst brands, so technologically, they look quite similar. Ariel, which contains 'bioenzymes', is a microsystem. Surf Ultra contains 'stain digesters'. These are these brands' USPs. Promise toothpaste, which contains 'clove oil', has this as a strong USP. Mere promises are not enough—they must be rationally justified.

Third, consumers tend to remember just one strong claim or concept from an ad. The claim should be strong enough to pull new customers to the product. Maggie Two-Minute Noodles revolutionised children's eating habits. Its USP is the short time required to cook it, and so, instant gratification for a hungry child.

Brand Image

Ad guru David Ogilvy's best-known concept is brand image. Advertising has to invest any brand with a set of associations, favourable connotations and positive psychological overtones. Mostly, these are not intrinsic parts of the brand, but add-ons. They are intangible attributes and not real qualities. The brand is given certain distinctive associations to bring out its distinct identity, by the advertising agency. These associations stimulate the fantasies and aspirations of the target market. If we see Marlboro cigarettes, we immediately associate them with carefree cowboys ... freedom ... muscle power ... the mythical West. These are perceptions that have been built around the brand USP and brand image differ in one aspect. The first appeals to logic and rational thinking. The second holds psychological and emotional appeal. Every rational appeal needs an emotional trigger. Even appeals like economy are expressed through emotionally charged lines, such as 'Surf Ki Kharidaari Mein Hi Samajhdari Hai', with

Lalitaji congratulating herself on being a thrifty housewife. So, appeals are a mix of reason and emotion.

Copywriting: Press Advertisements

"Copywriters devising selling ideas are recommended to follow the advice of Andrew Marvell to his coy mistress: "Let us roll all our strength, and all/Our sweetness, up into one ball ..." The selling idea should communicate quickly and clearly. It should also go on communicating. It should not be something of which we grow tired. It should have the potential of becoming part of the language, part of the culture".[7]

There are a few tools that are commonly used for creating a good ad. These are like the chisel and the mallet and give ideas meaningful shape. Important elements in print advertising are:

- The headline
- The visual
- The text/body copy
- The logo
- The baseline.

Creative brilliance can make or mar the success of a brand. It contributes a great deal to brand equity.

David Ogilvy said that an advertisements that sells was of more importance to marketers than anything else. He said, "When I write an advertisement, I don't want you to tell that you find it creative. I want you to find it so

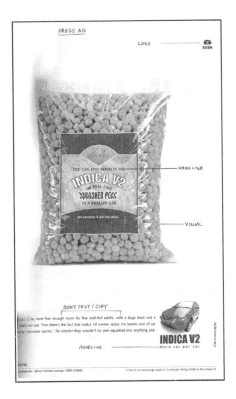

interesting that you buy the product." Who can deny that Ogilvy's copy for Rolls Royce, "At sixty miles an hour, the loudest noise in the new Rolls Royce comes from the electric clock", is a wonderful creative line that sells, too.

A vast amount of time, money and energy go into the creative work of developing advertising that influences the buying behaviour of consumers. The basic concepts in marketing tell us that it is all about satisfying consumer wants and needs. All appeals are created for the purpose of advertising human needs and wants and projecting how the advertised brand can satisfy those needs and wants. A.H. Maslow put together a basic human need structure in five hierarchical levels:

- *Physiological needs:* Biological needs, the most potent of all human needs, such as food, water, sleep, hunger and thirst
- *Safety needs:* The need for physical safety, security and stress
- *Love needs:* Needs such as affection and that of belonging, partially fulfilled by marriage and parenthood
- *Esteem needs:* The need for self-respect, prestige, social approval and achievement
- *Self-actualisation needs:* The need for self-fulfilment, aesthetic satisfaction and acquiring knowledge.

Aesop Glim wrote a simple book, titled *How Advertising is Written and Why,* in which he explained the secret of successful copywriting, relying on nine basic appeals—the five senses of sight, hearing, touch, smell and taste and the four instincts of sex/love, anger/rage, fear/security and hunger.

Security

न गीला. न ढीला.

देखो !

नया हगीज़ ड्राय - फिट डायपर मेरा सबसे अच्छा दोस्त है। इसके अनोखे डबल लीक बेरियर गीलेपन को बाहर नहीं आने देते हैं। इसका सुपर एब्जॉर्बेंट मटीरियल गीलेपन को फौरन सोख लेता है। तभी तो ना गीला ना ढीला, मम्मी भी आसानी से पहना सकती हैं।

नया

HUGGIES

M

त्वचा रहे ज़्यादा सूखी, ज़्यादा स्वस्थ.

Fear

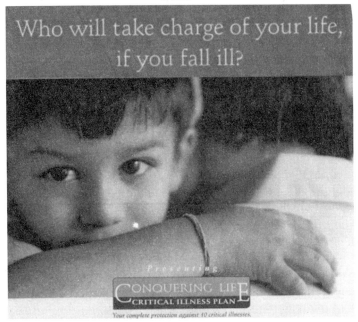

Hearing

Hunger

Touch

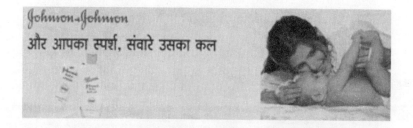

Sight

Taste

Smell

Strong Bonds
Strong Taste

*Cherish the **dumdaar** flavour!*

We can see the way these appeals are used in these headlines:

- *Looks so nice, wish I could keep it in the drawing room (Sight).*
- *Works without a whisper (Sound).*
- *My cotton sheets come out feeling like silk (Touch).*
- *The fresh aroma of clean sheets (Smell).*
- *Looks good enough to eat (Taste).*
- *Darling, you are glowing, let's eat out tonight! (Love/Sex)*
- *My husband wanted a divorce ... then I got a washing machine (Anger/Rage).*
- *Who's afraid of turmeric stains? (Fear)*
- *Mummy, these fritters are yummy! (Hunger)*

Writing Headlines

Jim Aitchison, an eminent advertising master said, "The written word is the deepest dagger you can drive into a man's soul." The most crucial part of advertising is the headline. Basically, a headline is used to arrest attention and to create interest. Headlines contribute immensely to the style and mood of an advertisement. Self-interest is the key to successful headlines. We would like to know what benefits a product offers us or what solution a company has for our problems. A black and white ad featuring a photograph of a man who appears to be pregnant is considered the best press ad of all time because of its innovative appeal and big idea. It was published in the late 1960s for the UK Health Education Council.

Would you be more careful if it was you that got pregnant?

For advice and answers to questions on birth control, contact The Family Planning Association of Victoria or your local doctor.

The Family Planning Association of Victoria, 259 Church Street, Richmond 3121, Telephone: 029 1177

Basics of Writing Headlines

- They should suggest a quick and easy way out. We still remember the headline of a hormone cream: *'How Women over 35 Can Look Younger'*.

- Self-interest should be created in every headline. Ciba's Otrivin nasal decongestant says: *'When You Cannot Smell a Rose'*.

- There should be news in the headline. People are always on the lookout for new or improved products. So, headlines use words such as 'Introducing', 'Announcing',

'For the First Time in India', 'Never Before', 'New!', 'Today's'.

- The headline should always target the prospective buyers. Thus, *'Free for Students!'*, *'Housewives under 30 May be Pleased to Know'*, *'Senior Citizens are Eligible for Half-Rate Airfares'*.

- Many people read the headlines. All of them may not read the rest of the copy. So, it is good sense to use the brand name of the product in the headline.

- The copywriter has to be imaginative in coining new words or phrases in the headline. A good example is Lacto Calamine's headline: *'Skinnocence'*.

- An element of curiosity in the headline prompts the buyer to read further.

- An attempt should be made to make the headline memorable.

- Effective headlines often modify and are modified by the visual: The headline and the visual work together to communicate one idea. Ads like the one for Nulon, in which the illustration of the hands under water was balanced by the apparently contradictory headline, *'Picture of a Lady Drying Her Hands'*, are good examples.

- Headlines with 'how', 'what' and 'why' in them do the trick in pulling in buyers: *'How to Remove Stains'*, *'Why She Wants Only a Garden Sari'*, *'How to Get Your Husband to Get Up Early'*.

Building the Body Copy

For generations, advertising copywriters have been taught that the most powerful words in the English language, or any language for that matter, are 'new' and 'you'. Words are their tools of trade, their only means of expression and persuasion. Explorer Ernest Shackleton's copy (*see below*) is arguably the best ad ever written. Every word has its own meaning and impact. It is very stark, compelling and challenging. The advertising writer needs, to a significant degree more than most other writers, the negative

capability that Keats praises. It is necessarily a very self-effacing kind of writing with one eye fixed firmly on the product and the other one even more firmly on prospective consumers. If there is one golden rule, it is: "Be sure every word is relevant to the reader and is understood by the reader".[8]

The emphasis on headline and picture is certainly not wrong. Sometimes, the visual is the main attention getter, sometimes the headline wins. Often the headline and the visual are so closely linked that the creative team would find it hard to say where the thought originated.

Essentials of Good Body Copy

- Research shows that if the first fifty words or so are able to fascinate the reader, it is likely that he will continue with the whole copy, be it another hundred words or a couple of pages. So, the copy should come to the point as quickly as possible, before the reader loses interest.

- Tell the truth: It enables the product to live longer in the market. The moment customers find that they have been cheated, the product is doomed to failure.

- You can always find an imaginative way of handling a product's weakness. This is by admitting the weakness of the product, but counter-balancing it with some unique positive features. For example, *The Times of India*, in one of its ads, says, *'We're No. 2. The No. 1 is Trying Harder'.*

- The more specific the message, the more attention-getting and memorable it is. Consumers want very specific factual information about the product. Copywriters must assume themselves to be in the consumers' shoes and look at the problem from their point of view.

- Testimonials from celebrities meet with a favourable response from consumers. But all endorsements should be credible. Good copywriters are always on the alert for little things that add conviction to the message.

- It matters whether the message is delivered in a personal way or in a generalised manner. A sincere personal tone gets more results.

- Deliver a simple message, instead of one that makes too many points. Simple language works like magic. Small words, small sentences and small paragraphs are the ingredients of successful copy. Friendly, enthusiastic copy keeps readers with it.

- Short copy is favoured, but there is no ban on long copy. In fact, for high-involvement products, longer copy is more desirable.
- Use evocative or figurative language to build a picture in the consumers' mind. While writing copy, an attempt should always be made to make the message memorable.

Writing for Television

The Testimonial

It is very believable when someone you know or admire appears on television and swears that Brand X is the only one for him, as,

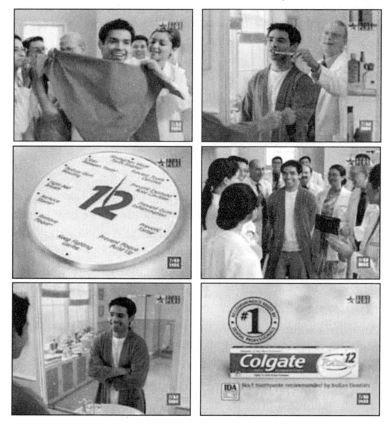

for example, cricketer Sachin Tendulkar for Visa credit cards and chess champion Vishwanathan Anand for NIIT.

Slice of Life

Real-life situations with which the viewer can easily identify—a mother-in-law—daughter-in-law scene or a child winning a race in school. The Wheel detergent powder ad, in which the husband is repairing his scooter, while his wife runs into the shop to buy the detergent, is a good example.

Humour

Humour can raise attention and memory retention. It can make a product friendlier and more approachable. But it must be relevant to the brand, as in the Krackjack or Fevicol ads.

Demonstration

Seeing is believing. Believability and credibility—the essence of persuasion—are high because we believe what we see. Clinic Plus anti-dandruff shampoo's ads are high on demonstrative power.

Musical Commercials

Ear-catching jingles always add to a product's recall power. The jingles become popular in themselves and the more people hum them, the more the brand power increases. A good example of jingles making a brand is Close-Up toothpaste's *'Kya Aap Close-Up Karte Hai?'*

Problem Solution

An instant solution is offered to the consumers' problem in the form of a product. This technique is as old as television. You show the viewers a problem with which they are familiar and then show how your product solves the problem. In the Dettol ad, a child is shown winning a prize for not falling sick and attending school

regularly. The reason why he does not fall sick is because Dettol keeps germs away from his home.

Computer Graphics

Computer graphics enrich a product's image in order to sell it vigorously. Take, for example, the Bajaj Pulsar ad, in which the motorbike moves automatically towards beautiful nurses. This holds appeal for young men, at whom the bike is targeted.

Comparison

This is not an often used tool, but could be very powerful in bringing out a brand's competitive edge, as, for example, in positing the features of an LG TV against those of a Samsung TV.

Writing for Radio and Multimedia

In the early 1920s, before the arrival of television, radio was king. People were glued to their radio sets, not just to listen to their favourite programmes, but also to hear the news of the world. Radio was so much a part of their lives that they set their watches by radio time. It was the backdrop for all domestic activities. Housewives went about doing their chores with the radio or transistor playing all day long, and cricket fans still depend on this aural and portable medium for the latest game scores.[9]

Tone of Voice

The most important element in radio advertising is the voices which are heard in jingles, spoken dialogues and announcements. Voices communicate much more than even facial expressions. We can use tone of voice to generate a mood or to impel action.

The Voiceover

Too many voices clutter up the message. The announcer's voice is enough if you have a strong line to deliver.

Voice Contrasts

If using more than one voiceover, try and introduce contrasts, whether man-woman, woman-child or high-pitched—low-pitched.

Signature Tune

A distinctive bar of music often gets associated with a brand, like those for Nirma detergent, Lifebuoy soap and Atlas cycles.

Sense of Humour

A touch of humour can put a smile on the faces of listeners and enhance the product communication.

Sound Effects/Nostalgic Tunes

These generate familiarity and can work wonders for the product.

Film Songs

Film songs always appeal to Indians, and the copywriter should take advantage of this. A good example is the Coca-Cola 'Aati Kya Khandala' ad.

Radio Programmes

Product manufacturers can sponsor radio programmes, as, for example, Cibaca Hit Parade and Close-Up Antakshari.

Writing for Posters and Direct Mail

Posters are common for impulse products and well-known brands that are widely distributed, bought by a broad cross-section of people and whose sales depend more on establishing awareness and a simple message, rather than a detailed comprehensive sales pitch. Direct mail, on the other hand, is often used by companies that have no other advertising apart from this very private medium for broad awareness. It is usually used for products for which that dimension is comparatively unimportant.

In terms of their creative exploitation, the two media are very different. Posters seek quick, memorable, slogan-based, primarily visual sales. In direct mail, the copywriter is king—words carry the burden of information and selling.

Guidelines for Good Posters

- *Encapsulate the copy strategy:* It is a medium for those who can communicate the heart of the copy strategy in one picture and about six words. The Formula toothpaste

poster is quite appealing with its visual and message, *'Builds Strong Teeth'*.

- *Identify the brand clearly:* As poster communication is limited, it is important that—at the very least—the brand is communicated.
- *Visible key words:* The lower third of many posters are often obscured by parked cars. Get the key message clear in the top half.
- Use clear, bright, primary colours on a white background to create an appealing look on a poster.
- *Be provocative:* Posters must be quick. While ads can take their time to identify the audience and involve them, posters need to shock you into attention.
- *Tie the poster into the overall campaign:* This means making the poster a summary of the written (press ad) and visual (TV ad) content of the whole campaign.

The most fundamental point in direct mail is the need for good writing that is able to engage the prospects' attention, interests and sympathy and provoke them into action. This is a medium that attracts punctilious, careful writers skilled in words. It is not a job for the superficial slogan writer.

Rules for Direct Mail

- Get the right address list and test it. The best direct mail campaign can only be as effective as the list of people to whom it is sent.
- Personalise the mail. Nowadays, the computer and the laser printer have made perfect personalisation possible.
- Mail copy is long and repetitive. It should repeat the main argument.
- Attempts should be made in the mail to involve the recipient.
- Make effective use of the envelope as a way to get the mail opened and by the right person.
- Encourage rapid response. Stimuli for quick response can include such things as a prize if you post back before a certain date, attractive conditions that lapse soon or that are open only to the first few respondents.
- Avoid duplication or conflicting messages in the mail.
- Plan repeat mail well. The mails should be seen as part of an ongoing campaign, not just a once-off, never-to-be repeated offer.

Notes

1. Valladares, June A., 2000. *The Craft of Copywriting*. New Delhi: Response Books, pp. 41–2.
2. Chunawala and Sethia, 2001. *Foundations of Advertising Theory and Practice*. Mumbai: Himalaya Publishing House, p. 6.
3. Hepner, H.W., 1961. *Advertising: Creative Communication with Consumers*. New York: McGraw Hill Inc., p. 6.
4. Young, James Webb, 1960. *A Technique for Producing Ideas*. Chicago: Crain Communication, pp. 25–41.

5. Barron, Frank, 1969. *Creative Person and Creative Process.* New York: Holt, Reinhart and Winston, p. 20.

6. Harrison, Tony, 1987. *A Handbook on Advertising Technique.* London: Kogan Page Ltd., p. 7.

7. Ibid., p. 88.

8. Ibid., p. 145

9. Valladares, June A., 2000. *The Craft of Copywriting.* New Delhi: Response Books, p. 220.

Three

The Sociolinguistic Base of Advertisements

> Language is intimately tied to man's feelings and activity. It is bound up with nationality, religion and the feeling of the self. It is used for work, worship and play by everyone, be he beggar or banker, savage or civilized. Because of its pervasiveness, it is the object of study by many branches of learning
>
> — Robert Lado

Sociolinguistics is a fascinating and challenging field of linguistics. It studies the way in which language interacts with society. Language is a social-cultural-geographical phenomenon—an integral feature of social behaviour. There is a deep relationship between language and society. It is in society that man acquires and uses language. When we study a language which is an abstraction of abstractions, a system of systems, we have to study its further abstractions, such as dialects, sociolects and idiolects. That is why we have to keep in mind the geographical area in which this language is spoken, the culture and society in which it is used, the context and situation in which it is used, the speakers who use it, the listeners for whom it is used and the purpose for which it is used, in addition to its linguistic components. Only then can our study of a language be complete and comprehensive. So, we must look at language, not only from within, but also from without, studying it from the points of view of both form and function.

Few of us are aware of the range and variety of our use of language in a typical day. Language will occur almost everywhere that we come into contact with other people and differ according to the nature of the contact. "It is impossible to fully distinguish language from the culture in which it appears. Nor can one speak of culture without speaking of its underlying values. And without some understanding of cultural values, one cannot appreciate the meanings of words as they are used in that culture".[1] In the United States, 'yes' means yes and 'no' means no because the Americans pride themselves on being blunt, practical and objective. But in Japan, interpersonal relations are often considered to be more important than objectivity, and vagueness and ambiguity are far more valued than bluntness of speech. So, in Japan, we rarely hear the equivalent of 'no', especially not if saying no might disappoint somebody. It has widely been noted that what is valued in a culture will be reflected in its language.

The scope of sociolinguistics, therefore, is the interaction of language and various sociologically definable variables such as social class, specific social situation, and status and roles of speakers and listeners. As J.B. Pride says, sociolinguistics is not simply an amalgam of linguistics and sociology; it incorporates, in principle at least, every aspect of the structure and use of language that relates to its local and cultural functions. Hence, there seems to be no real conflict between the sociolinguistic and psycholinguistic approach to language. Both these views should be reconciled ultimately.

Halliday writes, "In the development of the child as a social being, language has the central role. Language is the main channel through which the patterns of living are transmitted to him, through which he learns to act as a member of a 'society'—in and through the various social groups, the family, the neighbourhood, and so on—and to adopt its 'culture', its modes of thought and action, its benefits and its values".[2] The noteworthy feature is that it is the most ordinary, everyday use of language—with parents, brothers, sisters and friends in the home, in the street, in the park, in shops and in trains and buses—that serve to transmit to the child the essential qualities of society and the nature of social being.

Any study of language involves some attention to other disciplines; one cannot draw a boundary around the subject and insulate it from the others. Here, I am taking up the study of language under two headings: language with an inter-organism perspective (language as behaviour) and an intra-organism perspective (language as knowledge). Both these lead us outward from language as a system, the former into the region of sociology and other related fields, the latter into psychological studies. When we refer to 'social man', we mean the individual considered as a single entity, rather than as an assemblage of parts. The distinction we are drawing here is between the behaviour of that individual, his actions and interactions with his environment on the one hand, and his biological nature, in particular the internal structure of his brain, on the other. Language can be considered from either of these points of view, the first being what we called 'language as behaviour' and the second, 'language as knowledge'.

Language is the product of a culture. Throughout the world, English has many dialects such as British English, American English, Indian English, Canadian English and Australian English. There is no standard pronunciation that prevails everywhere for spoken English. But within this diversity, there is—more or less—a unity of grammar and one set vocabulary. Thus, each country that speaks the language can inject aspects of its own culture into the usage and vocabulary, but the broader frame of English remains the same.

Language with its different varieties is the subject matter of sociolinguistics. A regional, temporal or social variety within a single language is a dialect; it differs in pronunciation, grammar and vocabulary from the standard language, which is, in itself, a socially favoured dialect. So, a dialect is a variation of a language sufficiently different to be considered a separate entity within the language, but not different enough to be classed as a separate language. Sometimes, it is difficult to decide whether a variant constitutes a dialectal sub-division or a different language, since it may be blurred by political boundaries, as, for example, between Dutch and some Low German dialects. Regional dialects (or local or geographical or territorial dialects) are spoken by the people of a particular geographical area within a speech community, as, for example, Cockney in London, but are receding now due to increase in education and mobility of people.

Linguistic Diversity and Communication Patterns of a Tribal Society

Before planning the research design of this work, I was curious about the sociolinguistic setting of Arunachal Pradesh. Since I was employed in that state, I got an opportunity to observe closely its unique tribal society and its amazing linguistic ambience. Arunachal Pradesh lies at the foothills of the great Himalayas and has a common border with Tibet in the North, the great Brahmaputra valley of Assam in the South, China in the East and Bhutan in the West.

The total area of Arunachal Pradesh is 83,578 square kilometres and its total population is 10,91,000. The total literacy rate is 54.69 per cent; the male literacy rate is 64.07 per cent and the female literary rate, 44.24 per cent. The current sex ratio is 901 females per 1,000 males.

Since 1950, the state has been administered by the Central government of India. It was known as the North East Frontier Agency (NEFA) during the days of the British rule, and renamed Arunachal Pradesh on January 20, 1972. Politically, the state is divided into sixteen districts: East, West and Upper Siang, Lohit, Anjaw, Upper Dibang Valley, Dibang Valley, East and West Kameng, Twang, Lower and Upper Subansiri, Kurung Kumey, Papum Pare, Tirap and Changlang.

A good number of the tribes inhabiting this hilly state are of Mongoloid stock. The principal tribes are Adi or Abor, Nyishi or Dafla, Aptani, Tagin, Mishmi, Khampti, Nocte, Wancho, Tangsa, Singpho, Monpa, Sherdukpen and Aka. They speak distinct dialects, derived from the North Assam branch of the Tibeto-Burman sub-family of the Sino-Tibetan language stock.

The Tibeto-Burmans, whom anthropologists call Mongoloids, was a branch that spoke Sino-Tibetan. They were originally inhabitants of China, where they lived mainly along the banks of the great rivers of that country. They entered North-eastern India by following the Brahmaputra river around 2000 BC, parting company with their Tibetan cousins in the prehistoric period. The people who settled in Tibet and nearby places were known as the Bhot or Bot, while the people who migrated into Northeastern India were known as the Bodos.

Some allied groups of these settlers entered Myanmar (earlier known as Burma) along the Irrawaddy river and went further to Thailand. The migration of people from China to Northeastern India continued till the eighteenth century. The precise dates of these migrations are difficult to trace since dates have always been elusive in Indian history. But we know that the Thai-Ahoms came into Northeastern India in 1228 AD. They established the Ahom kingdom in Upper Assam and ruled there continuously for 600 years. The Thai-Ahoms claim descent from the Siamese or Thais, a branch of the great Sino-Tibetan people. Their secondary home was Myanmar.

Many of the Tibeto-Burman languages are spoken in the seven states of Northeastern India. Among these are Bodo, Rabha, Garo, Mishing, Meithei and Mizo, all of which belong to the Sino-Tibetan family. The Sino-Tibetan family has two principal divisions.

- Tibeto-Burman
- Thai Chinese

The Tibeto-Burman group is further divided into four main sub-groups:

- Himalayan
- North Assam
- Assam-Burmese
- Tibetan

In Arunachal Pradesh, the names of a tribe and its dialect are the same. The Adi (Abor), Nyishi (Dafla), Mishmi and Mishing belong to the North Assam sub-group of the Tibeto-Burman group of the Sino-Tibetan family. Adi has a number of distinct dialects. Mishing is an influential language that has two distinct varieties, one that is spoken in the hilly areas and another that is spoken in the plains. Hill Mishing bears a close affinity with Nyishi. The dialect that is spoken by each Mishing group bears a resemblance to th)se spoken by the others. Mishing is rich in folk literature, but has no writing tradition.

There are also other tribes living in Arunachal Pradesh, such as the Nocte, Tangsa, Apatani, Sherdukpen, Tagin, Monpa, Solung, Miju, Khowa and Singpho, each of which speaks a distinct dialect belonging to the North Assam sub-group. Among these, Nocte and Wancho are said to have affinities with the Bodo-Naga languages. Wancho is said to be similar to Konyak of the Naga branch. Solung is known to be closer to Nyishi. Miju and Aka sound similar. Monpa is said to be similar to Tibetan. One can see the influence of Kuki-Chin and Shan upon Singpho. Though there are around twenty-five tribes speaking about seventy dialects in the region, the question of distinguishing language from dialects does not arise at this stage. None of the dialects have any script, except Khampti, which uses a variant of the Shan script. The Monpas use the Tibetan script for their religious scriptures.

All human languages have the potential for being developed for all the purposes that human society and the human brain can conceive. They grow and develop by being made to function in newer contexts and newer interactional settings.[3] In a multilingual society like Arunachal Pradesh, English has a set of roles to play. It begins as a subject and is taught at all levels. From the primary school onwards, it is officially the only medium of instruction. It is used for interpersonal and inter-institutional communication in a wide range of contexts. It is used extensively in schools, colleges, universities, offices, secretariats and courts. Nevertheless, despite the increasing literacy and spread of education, English is not yet the language of the common man. But it does enjoy mass attitudinal support and is seen as a tool for promoting unity and gaining prestige.

The number and hierarchical ordering of languages differ from region to region. What we must guard against is getting into a 'pressure cooker syndrome', for excessive pressure might blow up the entire system. What is crucial for maintaining 'unity in the midst of diversity' is the philosophy underlying the 'salad bowl' image, in which each language has its characteristic features and yet contributes to the richness of the overall pattern.[4] In Arunachal Pradesh, Hindi, English and Assamese are used as the alternative means for intercultural and cross-cultural communication. In a state like Arunachal Pradesh, more than one language is needed for social mobility and cultural integration. As there are many tribes in the state, it is difficult for them to interact with each another in only one of the indigenous languages because each tribe has its own dialect, and sometimes, even more than one dialect.

In Indian linguistic settings, almost every state has one prominent, widely used language that all the people of that state speak and understand. This main language also works as a link language for interpersonal and intercultural communication in the entire state. Even a small piece of information, such as a general public notice, is written and circulated in this main language. It is rare that some other language is used for everyday needs. For example, in states such as Madhya Pradesh, Uttar Pradesh and

Rajasthan, the main or most favoured language is Hindi and all public notices, circulars, ads and tenders are communicated mostly in Hindi.

Arunachal Pradesh is unique in its linguistic diversity, sociopolitical system and geographical conditions. An advertisement for the national Pulse Polio campaign is disseminated in at least three languages—Hindi, English and the local dialect—here. Interestingly, the local dialects do not have a script, so the dialectal speech is converted into Roman form so that the local people can understand the ad in their own dialects. For example, the following ad, a popular communication, is disseminated thus:

English:	*Delay the First, Space the Second, Stop the Third*
Hindi:	*Pehla Jaldi Nahin, Doosra Abhi Nahin, Teesra Kabhi Nahin*
Adi:	*Kerong Kem Ogor Mapeka, Annyi Nanem Otom Langka, Angum Nape Oku Mapeka*

Since there is still a sizeable population that does not understand Hindi and English, such multilingual campaigns help them to understand the essence of the ads. Government advertisements and information of public interest need wide publicity and mass support in propagating their message effectively. The publicity of such multilingual advertisements is a symbol of effective administration. It affects public awareness and the social mobility of the masses immensely. It also makes people aware of their social welfare and political rights. Therefore, such multilingual ad campaigns make the communication task more easy and widespread. It is a better way of reaching all the people of the state, irrespective of linguistic barriers.

The Adis are numerically the largest group of people inhabiting the East, West and Upper Siang districts of Arunachal Pradesh. It has a number of sub-groups, such as the Gallong, Padam, Minyong, Bosi, Boker, Pasi, Pagi, Rame, Paillibo, Aashing, Tangam, Shimong and Karko. Each sub-group has some salient features with respect to customs and dialects of their own.

The Adis and other tribes have a rich folk literature, but in oral form. One generation passes it to the next by word of month in the absence of a script for written communication.

By now, the Roman script has been accepted to some extent by all the sub-sections of the Adi community for reading and writing. The existence of the Roman script dates back to British times, when it was introduced in the region for the smooth functioning of the government here. During British rule, Christian missionaries also promoted the Roman script in the Adi area as a part of teaching English. R.N. Koley, research officer in Arunachal Pradesh, finds many instances of the Roman script having been practised and popularised extensively for the Adi language by different segments of Adi society. He says that the Roman script is also popular because it has the advantage of enabling typing.[5] The All India Radio station of this area has done a remarkable job of promoting the Roman script: The AIR station broadcasts talks, stories, folk tales and folk songs in the Adi language, but makes it mandatory to submit the script of the programme before it is aired. This, naturally, happens in the Roman script.

Now efforts are being made by local bodies to record the *Aabangas* (the sacred Adi literature) in the Roman script. Many literary and cultural competitions take place during tribal festivals to encourage writing in the local language. These practices promote young artists and indigenous craftsmen and contribute to the enrichment of tribal arts and literature. Till the Adi and other tribes develop their own script, the Roman script serves as a practical alternative.

The local dialects, in conjunction with Hindi, English and Assamese, add more colour and excitement to the existing linguistic diversity of the tribal people, and such interactions among the languages in the form of influences and cultural borrowings tend to strengthen mutual comprehensibility and enhance the spirit of unity in diversity in the country.

PARENTS ALERT
POLIO IS A THREAT

BE WISE, IMMUNIZE

IPPI DATES
5th January 2003 & 9th February 2003

All children between 0-5 years of age must be immunised on the above two dates

Polio virus can lead to life long Paralysis of the limbs of your child

Your child can be a carrier of Polio even if he himself is protected against it

It's imperative to go for mass immunisation if Polio has to be eradicated from the world

by : Dept. of Family Welfare,
Govt. of Arunachal Pradesh
Naharlagun - 791 110

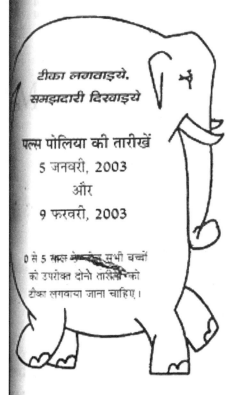

माता पिता ध्यान दें!
पोलियो खतरनाक है

टीका लगवाइये,
समझदारी दिखाइये

पल्स पोलिया की तारीखें
5 जनवरी, 2003
और
9 फरवरी, 2003

0 से 5 साल के बीच सभी बच्चों को उपरोक्त दोनो तारीखों को टीका लगवाया जाना चाहिए।

पोलियो वायरस से आपका बच्चा जिन्दगी भर के लिए **लकवे का शिकार** हो सकता है।

खुद आपका बच्चा पोलियो फैला सकता है, भले ही उसे टीका लग चुका हो।

दुनिया से पोलियो को मिटाना है तो व्यापक टीकाकरण जरूरी है।

Issued by Dept. of Family Welfare, Govt. of Arunachal Pradesh, Naharlagun - 791 110

INTENSIFIED PULSE POLIO IMMUNISATION

1st Round:Day 1: 05/01/03 (booth day)	2nd Round : Day 1 : 09/02/03 (Booth Day)
Day 2: 06/01/03 (h-t-h Visit)	Day 2 : 10/02/03 (h-t-h Visit)
Day 3: 07/01/03 (h-t-h Visit)	Day 3 : 11/02/03 (h-t-h Visit)

MAKE MY WORLD

POLIO

FREE

Bring All Children 0–5 Years
(Including Immunized and Sick)
On Both Round To
The Immunization Post, House to House Visit
Pulse Polio Doses are in Addition
To Routine Immunization

Published by: **District Health Authority, Pasighat**

INTENSIFIED PULSE POLIO IMMUNISA

5, 6, 7 TARIK JANUARY, 2003, DELOKKE 9, 10, 11 TARIK FEBRUARY, 2003

- POLIO MIMAK MOKOLO MOMIN GELANGKA.

- NOLUK KO KIDAR EM POLIO KUSERENG BIKO CENTRE LO GIBO LANGKA

- OLEN LOKKE ILA TAKNGOARALOK (0–5) KO (KERAPE BEJI-KUSERENG LAYINA DELOKKE KINA-RAMNA DONGKOM) KIDAR EM 5,6,7 TARIK JANUARY, DELOKKE 9, 10, 11 TARIK FEBRUARY, LO PULSE POLIO KUSERENG BIKO CENTRE LO ABO NANGKA.

- PULSE POLIO KUSEREHG SI BIYAR NAM POLIO KUSERENG ARELO BITAK SINAMKO.

Published by: **District Health Authority, Pasighat.**

"LEPROSY EM MOPI LADU"

1. LEPROSY HIGI MAJJABE NYOKGA HIMANAGO.

2. LEPROSY HIGI GIGE – SIGE MANAMGO OKKE YIRNE GONE GE YIRLIK MANAMGO.

3. LEPROSY SI TAPUM LOK NANNEGO.

4. LEPROSY SIM (MDT) MULTI DRUG TREATMENT EMNAM DOBAI LOK MOPI LADU.

5. LEPROSY EM GAKGOR LA DOBAI DOGOR YOM LETU-LAKTU DENAM MOTUM LADU.

6. AI APIN LO YAPU OKKE LISI NA ATAK GO GELA OKKE EGE ENPA, MABE IYOM, LEPROSY BE ILA DU. OGO DOCTOR EM BENA BE KATOM TOKA.

DISTRICT LEPROSY SOCIETY
EAST SIANH DISTRICT
PASIGHAT

SPREAD THE FACTS AND HELP FIGHT LEPROSY

- LEPROSY IS COMPLETELY CURABLE AT ANY STAGE.
- LEPROSY IS NOT DUE TO HEREDITY NOR BY CURSE OR SIN.
- LEPROSY IS CAUSED BY 'GERM'. IT IS NOT A HIGHLY INFECTIOUS DISEASE.
- MOST PATIENTS CANNOT SPREAD DISEASE.
- ONCE UNDER TREATMENT, NO PATIENT CAN SPREAD THE DISEASE AND A PALE SKIN PATCH OR LOSS OF SENSATION ON THE SKIN MAY BE LEPROSY. CONSULT YOUR DOCTOR.
- MULTI - DRUG TREATMENT (MDT) CURES LEPROSY IN A SHORT TIME.
- EARLY DIAGNOSIS AND TREATMENT PREVENT ULCERS AND DEFORMITIES.
- CONCEALED UNTREATED INFECTIOUS TYPE OF LEPROSY REMAINING IN THE SOCIETY IS THE SOURCE OF INFECTION.
- DEFORMITY IN LEPROSY PATIENT DOES NOT MEAN THAT HIS DISEASE IS INFECTIOUS TO OTHERS. DEFORMITY CAN BE PREVENTED.
- HELP IN THE CARE AND TREATMENT OF LEPROSY PATIENTS WITHIN THE FAMILY AND COMMUNITY.

We must Eradicate Leprosy. Let us help the Leprosy Elimination Programme with the spirit of active involvement and cooperation.

N.B.: For further information please contact to D.L.S. Pasighat

National Leprosy Elimination Programme (India)
DISTRICT LEPROSY SOCIETY
East Siang District : Pasighat
(Arunachal Pradesh)

Legangem Lukan Langka Delokke Leprosy Kinamem Motumdope Igul Langka

1. TAKAM LEPROSY KINAM SIM IPI LADUNG.
2. LEPROSY SIME PAP KAKOLOK DELOKKE ODONG LOK GEMANG.
3. LEPROSY SI TAPUM KOLOK LENDO, SI YAGOPE GIYON SIMANG.
4. KINA ALUM LOK SI GIYON SIMANG
5. KUSERENG DOLEN RODEM SIKENA KINA-LOKOM SI GIYON SIMAYE
6. AMILLO YASING NA ATAK KINA GENAMDE DELOKKE ASIK E KENSIYIMAPE INAMDE LEPROSY PE ILANGDO, DOKTOR EM DELO GIKAN GELANGKA.
7. MULTI DRUG TREATMENT (MDT) KUSERENG BIYEM KINAMSI MENANGPE AIDOKU.
8. KINAM EM GAGGOR LA KUSERENG DOYEM (ULCER) TAPE-TARE KINAM DELOKKE AMILE AYOT-ASOT SINAME KAMADO.
9. LEPROSY KINAMEM LESUP SINAMDE TAKAM LEGAPE AIMANAM PE IDO. DELOK KINAME GIYON SIDOKU.
10. AMILE LEPROSY LOK AYOT ASOT IGEKOLOK ABITLO GIYON SIMANG. AMILE AIMAPE IPENAM EMKOM ITUMLADO.
11. LEPROSY KINAM EM ITUMKOLO TAKAME IGUL LANGKA.

NGOLU LEPROSY SIME MOPITPE AIDO. KAJU NGOLU TAKAME LEPROSY MPITNANA PROGRAMME SO TOLNAMPE DELOKKE LEKOPE IGUL LAI.

NATIONAL LEPROSY ELIMINATION PROGRAMME DISTRCT LEPROSY SOCIETY PASIGHAT

Vivekananda Kendra (Arun Jyoti—Pasighat)

Lakjin Jinnam

Gite Kone duyar dungem, lekonem rune-pine mibom yalumnam delokke midayalumnam ager em gerbom ibom dope jdo. Hekenn longe ayem, momang tapet em tabungem mepaksi-pala midanam ayon atel lok gibom kupe aido.

Dekena longe hupak angkai-ngoluk among legape. Ingko ete ane gite-gite beliem lemo kunam legangem gite botte yana kamang. Minam ngotnam, ager-anam tabungem gite konem lemokolo ilik kupe aido.

No sinung kakot em bomjing-kajing langka; api-angem kekim dope lemo silangka-agike among legape. Nokgidang yekor em no payeamong sim turbum kebom nadope. Sinung mite ke tebo lounem, sikong jakboke jakbo lolatem gite beliem pinadong kupe, Kone lolatom sonsun nadokupe.

> Gerbom langka Gite koneke Aun legape
> Anki langka sine moneke aseng legape.
> Lutom nam ater so tabung doying dulikdung.
> — Sri Aurobindo

Ingkona ager ko ngolu geryedi be Bharat gitesok aun-abe delokke ediyanam legape iyepe emla mipang siyar molang si lakjjn si.

Raksha Bandshan Message

There are times in a nation's history when providence places before it ONE work, ONE aim, to which everything else, however high and noble in itself, has to be sacrificed.

Such a time has now arrived for our Motherland when nothing is dearer than Her service, when everything else is to be directed to that end.

If you will study, study for Her sake, train your body and mind and soul for Her service. You will earn your living that you may live for Her sake. You will go abroad to foreign lands that you may bring back knowledge with which you may do service to her.

> Work that She may prosper
> *Suffer that She may rejoice.*
> All is contained in that single advice.
> — Sri Aurobindo

May this Rakhi remind us that whatever we do must be for the development of mother Bharat.

Code Switching

Code switching and code mixing are well-known traits in the speech pattern of an average bilingual person in any human society in the world. No society is genuinely monolingual. That is why the regular use of two or more languages is a worldwide phenomenon. In Arunachal Pradesh, too, multilingualism is present in practically all classes of society.

When bilingual people speak to other bilingual people, they choose the appropriate language unconsciously, with no extra time or effort. There are numerous factors that account for language choice in a bilingual setting. Usually, it is a combination of several factors that comes into play when choosing one language over another. Ervin Tripp writes, "A speaker in any language community who enters diverse social situations, normally has a repertoire of speech alternatives which shift with the situation." There are considerable internal variations in the conversation of bilingual people. Speaker A does not always speak in the same way, nor does his interlocutor, B. This variation is easily detectable if you study their conversation closely. There is a variation in the extent to which the phonology, morphology and syntax of one language creep into the discourse of another language or vice versa. The speaker switches from one language or one language variety to another.[6]

Different scholars have defined code switching in different ways. Verma thinks of code switching as a "verbal strategy used by speakers in much the same way as creative artists switch styles and levels (that is, from the sublime to the mundane or the serious to the comic and vice versa). Or the ways in which monolinguals make selections from among vocabulary items. Each type of coding or code-switching is appropriate to the topical and situational features that give rise to it".[7]

Trudgill prefers to define code switching as "switching from one language variety to another when the situation demands".[8]

Grosjean defines code switching as" the alternate use of two more languages in the same utterance of conversation".[9]

To sum up, code switching is a communicative strategy in linguistic situations, in which two or more languages coexist within the bounds of one society or are kept in constant contact by politically and economically determined interests. The speaker switches from one communicative code to another under specific situations and normatively defined conditions (which are linguistic, psychological, social and pragmatic in nature).

Code switching has been used as a strategy to present a faithful picture of the linguistic performance of English-based bilingual people. "Hindi-English bilingualism has set in motion two processes—the English-isation or Anglicisation of Hindi and the Indianisation or Hindi-isation of English. Both Anglicised Hindi and Indianised English represent new varieties of language. They draw sustenance from the sociocultural setting of India and function as registral and stylistic devices in bilingual communities".[10]

We must not, however, forget that we are teaching and learning English in the sociolinguistic setting of India. English has its own phonological, syntactic, morphological and lexico-semantic systems. These systems have been functioning in our sociocultural and sociolinguistic setting for more than two hundred years. The systems of English have interacted with the systems of the major Indian languages. The cultural systems underlying English have interacted with the sociocultural systems underlying the major Indian languages. These interactions have generated a new variety of English with its own sub-varieties. In the process of using English, which has been a vehicle of Western culture, as a tool of Indian culture and the Indian pattern of life, we have been slowly but definitely reshaping the language. It is the setting that gives a language its distinctive colour and flavour.

Today, Indian advertisements are a good example of code switching between Hindi and English and its wide popularity among the people of India. More and more Indian language words are creeping into headlines and slogans. This is a sign of the times and a reflection of how English is evolving and adapting to Indian culture and thought. This evolving language, Hinglish, resonates with the youth, who are looking for an identity for themselves. Youngsters are relieved to find a language with which they can identify. Hinglish is neither too Indian to embarrass them, nor too Western to alienate them. Both Indian desi brands and multinational brands use Hinglish to communicate their selling propositions.

In India, Amul butter is a pioneering brand that capitalises on this fusion and sets a new trend in the designing of advertising messages. Amul ads are memorable for their funny, lovely and topical representations of ideas in Hinglish. I think there is no one who has not relished these witty and humorous ads packed with tongue-in-cheek one-liners and served with Hinglish puns. When Tata Motors unveiled the Nano, the world's cheapest and most cost-effective and technologically advanced car, Amul butter took the opportunity to showcase itself in Nano-light.

The multinational cola brand, Pepsi, gave its global *'Ask for More'* campaign a Hinglish flavour in India with *'Yeh Dil Maange More'* ('The Heart Wants More'). Coca-Cola coined its own Hinglish slogan: *'Life Ho To Aisi'* ('Life Should Be Like This'). UK insurance giant Aviva's 'Forward Thinking' global campaign became *'Kal Par Control'* in India.

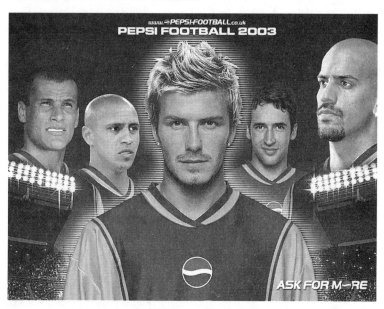

We see a lot of Hinglish in both Indian films and Indian ads. The Hindi version of Gurinder Chadda's *Bend It Like Beckham* was called *Football-Sshutball Hai Rabba*. Kurkure used the tagline, *'Chai Shai Mast Ho Jaye'*. Domino's Pizza asks its customers *'Hungry Kya?'* ('Are You Hungry?'). McDonald's invites you to come up with a new excuse in its Hinglish campaign, *'What Your Bahana Is?'*

(*Bahana* means excuse in Hindi, so the tagline is asking, 'What's your excuse for eating McDonald's and not home-cooked food?'). Along with being cool, Hinglish advertising messages make perfect business sense because they provide down-to-earth business communication to connect with a diverse audience.

Some other popular ad lines of this nature:

- '*Meethe Pal Phir Se*' (Equal low-calorie sweeter)
- '*Mirchi Sunnewale Always Khush*' (Radio Mirchi)
- '*Life Jam Jaye*' (Godrej Penta Cool refrigerator)
- '*Ho Jaye Dil Ka Connection*' (Kwality Wall's ice cream)
- '*Thodi Si Pet Pooja*' (Perk chocolate)
- '*Banaye Andar Se Strong*' (Dabur Chyawanprash)
- '*Hajama Fit Sehat Superhit*' (Zandu Pancharisht)

Highlighting the Indianness of Indian English, Gumperz says, "An Indian may speak English with control, he may read it, write it and lecture in it with great success. But when he uses English

Kwality Walls   *Ho Jaye*
Dil ka connection

in India, his speech will share some of the features of the other Indian codes with which English alternates in the daily round of activities. Indian English will thus deviate considerably from the norms current among the native speaker of English in the American Midwest. This kind of deviation represents not a failure to control English, but a natural consequence of the social conditions in the immediate environment in which Indian English is spoken".[11]

Register mixture is an important characteristic feature of certain varieties of language. In some cases, it is done consciously, in others, it just happens. Two or three different registers are mixed in order to heighten the effect of the discourse or create humour, or both. Leech refers to a concept called 'role borrowing'. He says, "Role borrowing is the use in one role of linguistic features appropriate to another. In private colloquy, its intent may be comic or sarcastic, in literature, it can serve various artistic purposes, in humorous writing or comedy entertainment, it is a form of parody. In advertising, role borrowing is just one aspect of the versatility of linguistic performance allowed within the situation".[12]

Verma offers an interesting example of the inter-language mixing of registers in which Hindi speakers use the phonological and grammatical patterns of Hindi with the lexical fillers derived from an English register. We will consider the following: "*Isse* dissection table *par le jao. Pehle isse* dissect *karna. Phir iske* veins and arteries *nikalna aur unki* microscopic examination *karna, baad mein unhe* refrigerator *mein rakh dena.*"

It is quite common today for speakers of Hindi and other Indian languages to switch to English when talking about abstract scientific principles or describing the working of some complex machinery. They use different varieties of their mother tongue in various situations in life, but when they have to use the technical register, they normally switch to English. This kind of register-oriented bilingualism may be labelled 'registral bilingualism'.

Some examples of Hindi-English mixed phrases in the different spheres of everyday life are: saving bank *khata, adarsh* deposit, *bachat* bank, *khata jama parchi, janana* ward, *mardana* ward and filmotsav.

One fear that has been voiced is that a highly Sanskritised or Persianised Hindi leads to the creation of an elitist language, while an English-Hindi mixed code leads to the birth of different varieties of pidgin Hindi and pidgin English. This fear is based on the false assumption that language is a monolithic system which can and should be carefully preserved in a glasshouse away from the reach of other languages. Today, Hindi has some stylistic varieties such as Persianised, Sanskritised, Anglicised and 'nativised' Hindi, each of which is used according to the topic of discourse, addresser-addressee relationship and sociocultural setting. We must remember that what sounded odd and funny yesterday sounds normal and familiar today. 'Classicalisation' and modernisation and tradition and modernity do not represent 'polar opposites'; they are mutually defining strategies used by human languages to capture 'the universe around us'.

Code mixing, as we know, is quite prevalent in advertising language. Copywriters understand their target audience and design an ad to serve their purpose of selling the product. Hindustan Petroleum (HP) gas' recent ad shows remarkable code mixing. No kitchen works without cooking gas. The HP gas ad touches the right chord among Indian housewives by promising them accurate gas weight in each HP cylinder. The ad goes:

Promise yehi

Weight sahi

HP Gas—Your Friendly Gas

In the ad for its CD Dawn motorbike, Hero Honda sells the bike as a cost-effective alternative to crowded public transport, posing it as *the* public transport for all people. The ad was obviously successful because Hero Honda advertised the large number of CD Dawns it had sold within a very short time of its launch. The ad says:

100 Days,

100,000 Bikes

Celebrating a Record Breaking Achievement

Hero Honda CD-DAWN

PUBLIC KA NAYA TRANSPORT

HERO HONDA

CD-DAWN

Value Naye Zamane Ki

We multilingual Indians tend to translate from one language into another, instead of thinking in just one particular language. That is why we hear phrases like 'I am going to go', 'You are eating my head', 'Don't do kit-kit man' and 'Rain is coming'. As translation equivalents of corresponding expressions in Indian languages, they are highly idiosyncratic and arbitrary. They are not deviations, but arbitrary creations—they have been created in the process of finding translation equivalents of concepts and ideas deeply rooted in Indian culture, faith and beliefs. Many Indian English writers such as R.K. Narayan, M.R. Anand and Khushwant Singh know the conventions of the standard dialect, but deliberately choose not to follow them. Their creations are motivated by their desire to make English an effective tool of Indian culture. Translation is a difficult and complex process. The greatest problem is to catch the right mood, tone, intention, feeling and sense of the original writer. An ideal translation is a perfect match of phonological, morphological, syntactic and semantic equivalents.

In the world of advertising, translation does a great job in circulating one ad in different languages. Copywriters are intelligent people and they take the utmost care while translating an ad from one language to another. Here are some examples:

- '*Aao Banaye Ek Behtar Kal*'
  - ▸▸ Let's Make Things Better' (Philips)
- '*Heera Hai Sada Ke Liye*'
  - ▸▸ Diamonds are Forever' (De Beers)
- '*Hum Isse Kahte Hai Manviy Takniki*'
  - ▸▸ We Call It Human Technology' (Nokia mobiles)
- '*Hai Aap Mein Woh Josh, Woh Junoon?*'
  - ▸▸ Do You Have It In You?' (Indian Army)

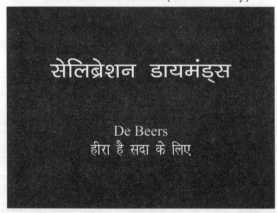

सेलिब्रेशन डायमंड्स

De Beers
हीरा है सदा के लिए

Two types of switching happen in Indian English. First, single lexical items or phrases are switched without any change from the background language to English, for instance, *sammelan, bandh, dharna, krishi*, etc. Most of these words restrict their meaning while being switched. Second, a word is taken from an

Indian language and mixed with English. Kachru calls this word formation process 'hybridisation'. In hybridised formations, the words comprise elements from both English and Indian languages. These formations then become a part of the English grammatical system of Indian English. Examples are *lathi-charge, gheraoed, filmotsav, bidi-smoking, city kotwali, rail-gaadi*. The plural words, *goondas* and *chakkis*, for example, are composed of code-switched words plus the English plural suffix, '-s'. Among the English affixes commonly used with Indian language words are 'ex-', 'non-', '-dom', '-ism', '-hood' and '-ic', like ex-rajas, goondaism and sadhuhood.

In India and other multilingual countries, English has been abundantly enriched by the multicultural, multiethnic and multilingual contexts in which it is used and the code switching that is used by non-native speakers to 'nativise' it.[13]

Code switching is the reality of any multilingual society. As a multilingual country, India is not an exception. Hindi-English code switching has produced a new language variety called Hinglish, which is widely practised. This trend is quite noticeable in both the electronic media and in advertising messages. There are purists who consider this mixed language to be a corrupt one and maintain that it should not be used in polite society. There are others—young learners and copywriters—who regard these varieties as natural and living extensions of the language as it exists.

The Sexist Language of Advertisements

In today's market, the most important job is to grab the consumer's attention and stimulate desire or action. We know that market forces thrive on the logic of what sells best and quickest. There is little doubt that sex fascinates us all, but to the businessman and the advertiser, it has an added dimension of interest—it sells.[14] When used well, it is a powerful technique that attracts, communicates, persuades and is remembered. Advertisers bank heavily on the use of sex, which is one of the most basic instincts of humans, to arouse and motivate them favourably towards the brand. The element of sex is evident in many ads.

Following the principle of no publicity is bad publicity, today, advertisers and manufacturers seem to use skimpily clad women to sell even handbags. While some parts of their target audience may actually love the eye candy on offer, others will remember the campaign for being outrageous. In either case, it is the company, the brand and the product that grab all the attention. So, its a win-win situation for all concerned.

As a broad umbrella term, 'linguistic sexism' covers a wide and diverse range of verbal practices, including how women are labelled and referred to and how language strategies in mixed sex interactions may serve to silence or depreciate women as interactants.[15] Cameron defines 'sexist language' as language that contains a lexicon and a grammatical structure that excludes, insults or trivialises women.[16] With respect to the representation of women in advertisements, the advertisers reinforce and obtain public sanction for certain value codes, which will serve their interests and create more profit. They subtly design the ad copy and create a world in which the brand is the hero and all other aspects are ordinary.

Sexual messages can be either verbal, in the form of spoken or written words, or pictorial, in the form of still or moving images. Verbal sexual advertising can be divided into two categories: erotic language and sexual innuendo. In practice, these forms often combine and are used along with pictures. Advertisers often employ puns in messages when they want to suggest indirectly things that are too indecent to be said outright. The following ad line, which is a tagline for honeymoon destinations, creatively employs linguistic ambiguity to enhance the impact of the message: *'After You Get Married, Kiss Your Wife in Places She's Never Been Kissed Before'*.

The tagline can be interpreted to mean that the husband is being asked to kiss his wife on parts of her body where she has never been kissed before. This would qualify as an indecent interpretation. The other—intended—interpretation points out that the husband should kiss his wife in locations where she has never been before.

Advertisements that contain sexual hints or flirtatious language are widely seen in both electronic and print media. Sex has been used globally to sell all kinds of products, including flowers. In one breast enlargement commercial in China, a woman with small breasts walks by, while a man is heard saying, *"Too small to be good"*. Another woman with bigger breasts shows up and the man shouts, *"Bigger is better"*. Such advertising messages reflect discrimination and disrespect for women. They reduce the entity of a woman to a mere 'body' or a saleable sex commodity. Even as a section of the media and public lambasts advertisers and ad agencies for the falling levels of taste and decency in advertising, such ads continue to hit the eye.

In April 1997, French Connection began branding its clothes *'fcuk'* (usually written in lowercase). Over the years, it has come up with various product ranges such as fcuk T-shirts and fcuk colognes. Initially, it caused furore in the media, with some newspapers commenting that "it undermined the fabric of society", but the company insisted that it was an acronym for French Connection of United Kingdom.[17] Despite being hauled up by the Advertising Standards Authority, the fcuk advertising proved to be a major hit. fcuk is just a very clever way to make the name stick in people's minds because it is associated with another four-letter word beginning with 'f'. French Connection fully

exploited this and produced an extremely popular range of T-shirts with messages such as *'fcuk this'*, *'hot as fcuk'*, *'mile high fcuk'*, *'too busy to fcuk'*, *'lucky fcuk'*, *'Fun Comes Usually Kneeling'* and *'fcuk on the beach'*.

While this was the trend the world over, India was not too far behind. We had the first Liril girl, Karen Lunel, in a lime-green bikini, frolicking under a waterfall and Milind Soman and Madhu Sapre wearing nothing but white shoes and a python for Tuff shoes. Indians may live in the happy belief that we cannot have sexuality in public media, but this is a myth. Female nudity and erotic content have become commonplace in current advertising.

The headline of the ad for Moods dotted condoms exploits this rhetorical device very well: '*The only time she will love friction in a relationship*'. Messages for contraceptives usually highlight the thrill and romance attached to lovemaking and avoid making people aware of the necessity of safe sex and the benefits of birth control. The Kamasutra headline goes: '*The Tough Part isn't Getting Her to Say Yes. It's Getting Her to Stop Saying Yes*'.

Another contraceptive brand, Moods, has a very inviting line:

> *Tonight*
> *Let it just be*
> *You & me.*
> *And nothing*
> *In between*

These messages are often found to be offensive to public decency and have severe consequences for the youngsters who represent our country. The Zaroor condoms headline, '*Kaun*

Jaane Kab Kahan Aur Kaise Dil Ki Chahat Poori Ho Jaye' ('Who Knows When, Where and How You'll be Able to Fulfil Your Heart's Desire'), shows that the ad world is treading where it dared not before in creating sexist, selfish, aggressive, insensitive male chauvinists. The headline seems in bad taste, quite overt and offensive. It depicts the image of women poorly and goes against the social and cultural norms of Indian society. The ad ends with the reminder: *'Hamesha Rakhe Saath'* ('Keep with You Always'). This trend is towards increasing eroticism and nudity in the media. Some women's groups have criticised the ad, arguing that it showed an unrealistic and sexually available woman. The ad contains an open sexually suggestive message and combines with the visual to heighten the image of a sexually driven woman who is on the prowl for a man. The advertisers think that they are showing women in a position of authority, but women say the ad depicts them as sexual objects.

Advertisements also exhibit the prevalent norms and customs of a society. A big Tanishq jewellery hoarding in Patna a few years ago said: '*Buy 24 Carat Gold and Let Your Daughter Stay in Peace at Her Sasuraal (marital home)*'. The emphasis was on the dowry system that exists in India. Technically, there's nothing wrong in the message, but advertisers should refrain from encouraging such practices in public.

Fighting as they are for more viewer ratings and greater consumer attention, advertising messages and images get dominated by factors of economic interest rather than those of customer satisfaction and sustainable communication. In the truest sense of the word, culture is being commodified and viewed as a cost-benefit factor for the attainment of a global media audience and a global information society. Things are similar in the Indian market. We often see images of pretty, teenaged girls in ads for products with which they have no connection. Impressionable and inexperienced pre-teenagers and teenagers are targeted unrelentingly with too many inappropriate, highly sexualised advertising images, including portrayals of kissing, dating, lovemaking and overt sexual behaviour. The advertising industry is using younger and younger models and now commonly portrays thirteen and fourteen year olds as men and women. Foreign brands such as Levi's, Calvin Klein, Axe, Gucci and Guess are offenders in this context. These ads are not selling products, but adult sexuality to young consumers.

Critics argue that advertising is more propaganda than information. It creates needs and highlights faults consumers never knew they had. Ads suggest that children won't succeed without a computer, that our bodies should be leaner, our faces younger and our houses cleaner. They point to the sultry, scantily clad bodies used in ads to sell everything from perfume to beer to power tools and argue that advertising promotes materialism, insecurity and greed.[18]

Notes

1. Cordon Jr., John C., 1975. *Semantics and Communication*. New York: Macmillan Publishing Co. Inc., p. 41.
2. Halliday, Michael, 1978. *Language as Social Semiotic*. London: Edward Arnold Ltd., p. 9
3. Verma, Shivendra K., 1993. *Aspects of English Language Teaching*. Chennai: TR Publications Pvt. Ltd., p. 112.
4. Ibid., p. 107.
5. Koley, R.N., 2000. 'Quest for Development of Adi Language', in *Arunachal Review*. Vol. 4, No. 28 (March-May). pp. 11-4.
6. Malik, Lalita, 1994. *Sociolinguistics*. New Delhi: Anmol Publications Pvt. Ltd., pp. 1-2.
7. Verma, Shivendra K., 1976. 'Code-switching: Hindi-English', in *Lingua*. 88 (2), p. 156.
8. Trudgill, P., 1980. *Sociolinguistics: An Introduction*. Harmondsworth: Penguin Books., p. 82.
9. Grosjean, Francois, 1982. *Life with Two Languages: An Introduction to Bilingualism*. Cambridge: Harvard University Press, p. 145.
10. Verma, Shivendra K., 1993. *Aspects of English Language Teaching*. Chennai: TR Publications Pvt. Ltd., p. 110.
11. Gumperz, J.J., 1964. Proceedings of the Ninth International Congress of Linguistics: Hindi-Punjabi Code-switching in Delhi. London: Mounton & Co.
12. Leech, Geoffrey W., 1966. *English in Advertising*. London: Longman Green & Co. Ltd., p. 110.
13. Malik, Lalita, 1994. *Sociolinguistics*. New Delhi: Anmol Publications Pvt. Ltd., p. 29.
14. Gallup-Robinson, 2006. 'Sex in Advertising'. Retrieved on August 6, 2006, from http://www.gallup-robinson.com/essay2.html.
15. Atkinson, K., 1993. 'Language and Gender', in S. Jackson et al., (eds): *Women's Studies: A Reader*. Hertfordshire: Harvester Wheatsheaf.

16. Cameron, D., 1985. *Feminism and Linguistic Theory*. New York: St Martin's Press.
17. 'Time Called on FCUK Posters'. 2001. BBC News. *http://news.bbc.co.uk/1/hi/uk/1258961.stm*.
18. Belch, George E., and Michael A. Belch, 2003. *Advertising and Promotion*. New Delhi: Tata McGraw-Hill, p. 751.

Four

The Psycholinguistic Base of Advertisements

First guy (proudly): "My wife's an angel!"

Second guy: "You are lucky, mine is still alive."

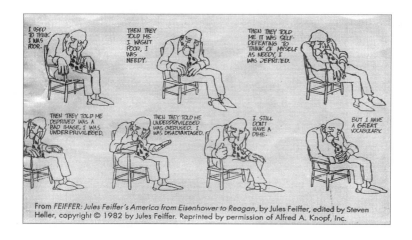

From FEIFFER: Jules Feiffer's America from Eisenhower to Reagan, by Jules Feiffer, edited by Steven Heller, copyright © 1982 by Jules Feiffer. Reprinted by permission of Alfred A. Knopf, Inc.

As we have already seen, man is unique in his ability to transmit ideas through language and this quality distinguishes him, not only from other animals, but also from the machines which he himself has created. He is a social animal who uses language to communicate in such a way that it is indispensable to the maintenance of his culture. Language is essential to human society and reflects every facet of our attitudes and behaviour. It is central to our culture and, therefore, needs close and systematic study. The psycholinguistic study of advertisements helps readers understand the symbols of expression and nuances of meaning employed in advertising messages.

Language is the most powerful, convenient and permanent means of communication. Non-linguistic symbols such as expressive gestures, signals of various kinds, traffic lights, road signs, flags, emblems, codes, Braille, sign language and the symbols of mathematics and logic are also means of communication, but they are not as flexible, comprehensive, perfect or extensive as language. Language is the best means of self-expression. In the Aesthetis Clinic ad, the advertiser uses two different symbols, the first symbol for the problem of excessive hair and the second symbol for the solution of the problem. The message is executed quite creatively with two different symbols, but the actual

meaning is difficult to decipher unless readers read the linguistic message—'Permanent Hair Removal'—and connect it to Aesthetis Clinic. It is clear that signs may have layers of meanings and that they are not independent of their context. The meaning of a sign is not contained within itself, but arises from its interpretation and context.

When we talk about language as a system of communication, we are speaking of human language. Animals certainly have communication systems and they communicate in a variety of ways, but these are mostly primitive, instinctive and incapable of expressing a wide range of concepts. Dogs bark, cats mew. Dolphins, bees and ants have probably the most sophisticated animal communication systems. Yet, compared with human language, their range is restricted to instinctive responses to their immediate environment. Animal communication is confined to certain basic contexts such as courtship behaviour, the rearing of offspring and fighting for territory or supremacy, or to situations in which cooperation within the species is desirable or necessary.

Human language is non-instinctive because it is acquired by human beings. Nobody gets a language in heritage, they acquire it—everyone has been provided with an innate ability to acquire language. Thus, while animals inherit their system of communication by heredity, humans do not.

Human language has creativity and productivity. It is this feature which enables the copywriter to persuade consumers to buy a product. While designing an ad, the copywriter brings together art and commerce. With the effective use of language, he makes pleasing and memorable ads and makes his point impressively in the marketplace. In the Horlicks ad shown here, the cute, chubby girl explains beautifully the secret of her well-being, while all her other friends suffer from one ailment or the other when the weather is bad. The copy is very creative and impressive and it serves the purpose of making the brand saleable and memorable. It doesn't invite consumers vigorously to buy the product, but smartly narrates the business message of how good it is to be a

"Sammy gets bad colds,
Jess gets fever,
Nell gets bad coughs,
Brian gets bad throat
and I get bored
on rainy days!"

Junior Horlicks consumer. *'Sell the sizzles, not the steak'* is another way of saying, *'Show, don't tell'*. People are always more mesmerised by sleight of hand than a documentary. It is human nature to want to escape from the humdrum into fantasy land. Advertising offers people a reason to be seduced. Sell them an idea, draw them a picture, invite them into paradise—even if it is only for a moment. They will come down to earth again when they actually use the product. Subconsciously, consumers expect this to happen.[1]

Advertising is all about persuading people. It needs the skills of selling to be translated to the right medium, whether paper or celluloid. People tend to believe what they see. The trick is to write copy that brings your client's product to life before your customer's eyes, even if they are sitting in their own homes. In a shop, customers get a chance to see what they are buying. Notice how people behave in a supermarket or a bazaar. If the product is not packaged, they tend to touch the tomatoes, squeeze them to judge their firmness and freshness. They smell the mangoes and papayas. They look and ask and feel before they decide to buy. This sort of behaviour annoys the shopkeeper, but the customers are not daunted.

In advertising language, the proposition is the message which the advertiser wishes to communicate to his target audience. Alyque Padamsee made it simple for the copywriter by putting it thus:

Proposition: Consumer Benefit + Reason Why

In other words, every advertising message ought to contain:

- A benefit to consumers
- A good reason for them to believe it is indeed so

This is one of the popular strategic approaches used by many brands, especially in highly competitive categories.

In the detergent category, for example, most brands claim a superior and whiter wash or superior stain- or dirt-removing abilities than the others because of their special product features. We can see it with washing machines: Whirlpool comes with *'agitator'* technology, LG with *'chaos punch'*, BPL with *'fuzzy logic'*, and IFB with *'tumble wash'*. Almost all brands talk of some or the other features that make them unique, different and saleable. Thus, the communication for LG TV sets talks about *'golden eye'*, Videocon TVs, about their *'bazooka'* feature, Onida TVs, about *'KY thunder'*, and so on. In the shampoo category, Clinic All Clear offers a *'ZPTO'* formula. Every brand

satisfies the same need as directly competing brands, but claims to do it better with its unique feature or benefit substantiation.

June A. Valladares writes, "Make USP the basis of all your advertising communication. In other words, when attempting to develop the proposition or message for your advertising (whether in print or in any other medium), you must give the target audience a benefit (what is in it for me?) and then a good reason to believe you (substantiate your promise)".[2]

The baseline for Lux soap contains just a few words, '*Beauty Soap of the Film Stars*'. But this baseline has remained unchanged for decades and has now become synonymous with Lux advertising all over the world.

When looking at the Lux toilet soap ad, we usually see a close-up of a beautiful film star's face, her soft and creamy complexion, a picture of the soap, a headline that is usually in the form of a testimonial from the star, signed off with the baseline: 'Beauty Soap of the Film Stars'. These are the elements that strike us immediately. The total advertising is the creative expression of the basic proposition, and the creative expression is the sugar coating with words and visuals on the proposition. The combination works so well that the potential buyer is persuaded to believe that Lux soap will immediately turn an ordinary face into that of a film star.

By now, it is evident that the present chapter concentrates on the psychological variables that govern consumer behaviour in buying a product. Companies that want to understand how consumers think and make decisions about products conduct sophisticated consumer behaviour research to identify their consumers, why they buy, what they buy and how they buy. Consumer behaviour, by definition, is the decision-making process and the physical activity of making a purchase.

"Advertisers often refer to core values when selecting their primary appeals. Because values are so closely tied to human behaviour and so difficult to change, private research firms try to monitor values and look for groupings of values and behaviour patterns. For instance, the importance of sending all children to college is emphasised in the US. Conversely, in Portugal, the custom is to send sons to college before sending daughters. So, ads for colleges in the US feature both men and women, while similar ads in Portugal feature mostly men."[3]

Many factors affect our response to an advertising message. Besides the culture and society in which we live, we have certain internal elements that make us individuals. The elements that shape our inner self constitute our psychological makeup. Although hundreds of different elements are encompassed under the term, 'psychological', the elements with the most relevance to advertising are perceptions, learning, motives, attitudes and lifestyles.

Perceptions

Each day we are bombarded with stimuli in the form of faces, conversations, news announcements, buildings and advertisements, yet we actually notice only a small fraction of these. Each person perceives a stimulus within his own frame of reference. The sheer number of stimuli to which we are exposed further

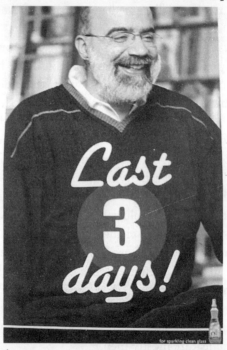

complicates the perception process. Some of these stimuli are perceived completely, some partially, some correctly and some incorrectly. Ultimately, we select some stimuli and ignore others because we cannot be conscious of all incoming information at one time. Another aspect of perception that is particularly germane to advertising is 'selective perception'. The process of screening out information that does not interest us and retaining information that does is called selective perception. This process occurs even when we watch television or read a magazine. It also occurs when we look at an ad and perceive only the headline, photograph or famous spokesperson. Looking at an ad for a glass cleaner, everyone receives its message in their own personal domain as perception depends on internal factors such as a person's beliefs, experiences, needs, moods and expectations. The ad's message, *'For Sparkling Clean Glass'*, can be understood in the context in which it is seen.

In addition to our tendency to select stimuli that are of interest to us, we also perceive stimuli in a manner that coincides with our reality. Our world includes our own set of experiences, values, beliefs, biases and attitudes. It is virtually impossible to separate these inherent factors from the way we perceive things. For example, we naturally tend to seek out messages that are pleasant or sympathetic with our views and avoid those that are painful or threatening. This is called 'selective disclosure'.

Similarly, when we are exposed to a message that conflicts with what we believe, we engage in 'selective distortion'. For example, a salesman may inform a consumer that a car does not have efficient gas mileage. But since the consumer has a strong desire to buy the car because of its heated leather seats and side air bags, he is likely to distort that negative point in order to conclude that the car is a good buy.

Our responses to stimuli have a direct bearing on advertising. A large part of what the brain processes is lost after just an instant. Even when we try to retain information, we are unable to save a lot of it. 'Selective retention' describes the process we go through in trying to save information for future use. Advertising can aid this process by using repetition, vivid images, easily remembered brand or product names, jingles, high-profile spokespersons, music and so on.

Another possible response to selective perception is a feeling of dissatisfaction or doubt. Seldom does a purchased product deliver all positive results. According to the theory of 'cognitive dissonance', we tend to compensate or justify the small or large discrepancies between what we actually receive and what we perceived we would receive. Advertising can play a central role in reducing this dissonance.

For the advertiser, selective perception and all its subcategories represent a formidable challenge. TV advertisers, for example, note that viewers tend to shift their perceptions as soon as commercials start. They may leave the room, change the channel, zap the commercials, converse with a family member or read a book. That is why the first five seconds of a commercial are so critical in capturing the perception (attention) of the viewer. Using a celebrity spokesperson, a cute puppy or kitten, a startling question or a half-naked girl are all attempts to hold the viewer's attention or perception.[4]

Learning

Perception leads to learning. We cannot learn something unless we have accurately perceived the information and attached some meaning to it. Learning is often an unconscious activity—consumers usually do not know it is happening. If advertisers understand how consumers learn, they can design ads that make it simple for consumers to learn the ad's key elements, such as brand name, product features and price. They can also tap into the different attitudes, beliefs, preferences, values and standards that affect learning and purchase behaviour.

Advertising prides itself on being ahead of the curve and helping to create and define popular culture. It expects us to learn new things and adopt what makes business sense. For example, in its bid to offer something hot and happening, it has showcased Valentine's Day for young people in India. Traditional Indian society does not approve of public displays of affection between the two sexes, including hand-holding and kissing. But advertising teaches youngsters how to celebrate Valentine's Day and buy gifts and cards for their romantic interest. If we look at advertising strategies, we find that marketing has never been so innovative: Valentine's Day ideas, Valentine's Day gifts, Valentine's Day cards, Valentine's Day songs and even Valentine's Day jewellery!

You cannot go to a restaurant now on Valentine's Day without getting plied with special dinners and special desserts for the occasion. The US Greeting Card Association estimates that around one billion Valentine cards are sent each year worldwide, making the day the second-largest card-sending holiday of the year after Christmas.

Various theories have been proposed to explain the different aspects of learning. Typically, experts rely on two approaches to understand the learning process. The first focuses on 'cognitive' or mental processes, the second on 'behavioural conditioning'. Cognitive learning theorists stress the importance of perception, problem solving

and insight. They characterise people as problem solvers, who go through a complex set of mental processes to analyse information. Advertisers who adopt the cognitive learning approach try to provide information that will help a consumer's decision-making process. The second school of theorists argues that people learn behaviour by experiencing connections between stimuli and responses through classic or instrumental conditioning. Essentially, classical conditioning pairs one stimulus with another that already elicits a given response, as in the experiments of Ivan Pavlov, in which a dog was trained to salivate at the sound of a bell by associating the sound of the bell with food.

When we repeat a process many times and continue to be satisfied with the outcome, we develop a habit. A habit is something that we have learned so well that it becomes second nature. A habit is a decision-making shortcut. We save time and effort because we do not evaluate the information about alternative choices. In addition, purchasing by habit reduces risk. Buying the same brand time and again reduces the risk of product failure and financial loss. Obviously, advertisers would like consumers to be habitual users of their products. Achieving that goal requires a powerful message backed by a superior product. For example, Coca-Cola successfully manages to portray itself as the only drink that has a terrific chilling effect. Not only the young people in India, but even toddlers know the message, 'Thanda Matlab Coca-Cola'. The word *thanda* has been communicated in such a way that the

lingering pronunciation (sound) itself gives a cooling soothing effect. In a similar way, another cold drink brand, Limca, associates itself with quenching thirst. Once a habit is formed, advertising should reinforce that habit through reminder messages, messages of appreciation and actual rewards such as coupons, premiums and rebates.

Advertisers use a number of techniques to improve learning. Music and jingles improve learning because they intensify repetitions. Creating positive associations with a brand name enhances learning. Testimonials by popular celebrities and scenes of attractive people in attractive settings also intensify positive associations. There isn't another outdoor campaign or mascot that's retained the ubiquity of a Gattu, the omnipresence of a Maharaja or the freshness of the Liril girl.[5]

An ad may also use humour because it gives the audience some reward for paying attention.[6] Almost all Amul butter ads have created positive associations with consumers by using humour. Amul's is the longest running hoarding campaign in the world—spanning almost four decades—and has even made it to the

Guinness Book of World Records. The Amul ads are topical, warm and witty. They make remarkable comments on current issues, whether related to sports, politics, festivals, seasons or films. In one of its film-based ads, which took off on a hit Hindi film of the time, called *Kabhie Khushi Kabhi Gham: It's All About Loving Your Family*, the baselines were converted thus:

Amul ads also use the popular Hinglish touch. Many of the ads are fine expressions of code switching that emphatically combine both Hindi and English to communicate the 'better butter' message. The ads based on the Sharjah cricket series in the late 1980s (*'Sharjah, Boys Match Haarjah'*) and Maradona (*'Mardona To Aisa Hona'*) exemplify the Hinglish touch Amul has given to Indian advertising. Jagmohan Dalmia, former president of the Board of Control for Cricket in India (BCCI), who was reportedly involved in a match-fixing controversy and unfair selection of players at the time, was a target of one controversial Amul hoarding: *'Dalmia Mein Kuch Kala Hai?'*

Apart from reaching out to a wider audience, the Hinglish messages tried to link the campaign with the product by making a social comment. Marketing gurus who believe that English words are central to the success of an ad line could take a cue from Amul's advertising campaign, which has proved the pundits wrong.

Motivation and Needs

We all have a level of personal motivation. A motive is an internal force that stimulates us to behave in a particular manner. This driving force is produced by the release of tension, which is caused by an unfulfilled need. People strive both consciously and subconsciously to reduce tension. At any given point, we are probably affected by a number of motives, some of which may be contradictory and some of which are stronger at certain times. For example, our motivation to buy a new suit will be much higher if we have several job interviews scheduled soon. Understanding buying motives is crucial to advertising because the advertising message and the timing of the ad should coincide with the consumer's motivation priorities. Garnier's 'Natural Technology for Healthy Beauty', which promises to get rid of pimples in just twenty-four hours works as a stimulant for teenaged girls who suffer from acne. The ad claims to introduce 'India's First Quick-Fix Pimple Control Pen', which is natural and healthy and provides a beautiful complexion.

Needs and wants are interdependent. All needs get manifested into wants, whether those needs come to the surface and get expressed or remain hidden. In that sense, wants are a conscious or subconscious expression of our needs. We are often more aware of our wants and able to articulate them better than our needs. Needs are one set of factors that influence whether we are motivated and how that motivation is manifested. Needs are the basic forces that motivate us to do something. Changes in consumers' lives often result in new needs and wants. Each person has his own set of unique needs. Some are innate, others are acquired. Innate needs are psychological and include the need for water, food, air, shelter and sex. Because satisfying these needs is necessary to maintaining life, they are also called primary needs. In the needs pyramid developed by psychologist Abraham Maslow, these are called physiological needs.

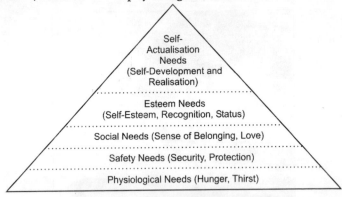

Maslow's Hierarchy of Needs

Acquired needs are those that we learn in response to our culture and environment. These may include needs for esteem, prestige, affection, power and learning. Because acquired needs are not necessary to our physical survival, they are considered secondary needs. Maslow called them social, egoistic and self-actualisation needs. Advertisers try to assess which needs are most important to consumers at any given time. However, no category of needs takes precedence consistently over the others. For example, since the events of September 11, 2001, safety and security have become overriding needs, especially in the US.

Attitudes

An attitude is a learned predisposition, a feeling that you hold towards an object, a person or an idea that leads to a particular behaviour. Attitudes tend to be resistant to change. We can hold an attitude for months or even years. Because attitudes are learned, we can change or replace them with new ones. Attitudes also vary in direction and strengths in that an attitude can be positive or negative, reflecting like or dislike, or it can be neutral. In a public-interest ad issued by BMW, the advertising message is used to create a favourable attitude towards safe driving and to advocate that drinking and driving should not go together.

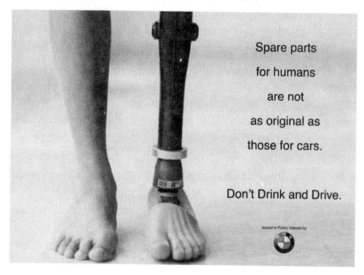

Spare parts
for humans
are not
as original as
those for cars.

Don't Drink and Drive.

Attitudes are important to advertisers because they influence how consumers evaluate products, institutions, retail stores and ads. We can change many lives and bring happiness by developing a positive attitude towards fearful diseases such as polio and HIV/AIDS. In an ad for HIV/AIDS awareness, film star Shabana Azmi appeals to people to be friendly and considerate towards people living with HIV. Actor Amitabh Bachchan warns society about the dangers of polio and asks parents to bring their children to polio booths to help eradicate the disease.

Psychographics

Researchers in marketing have combined demographics and psychological variables into a concept called psychographics. Advertisers are excessive users of psychographics because of its versatility and ability to create fairly complex consumer groupings. Lifestyle analysis is an extension to psychographics—it looks at the ways in which people allocate time, energy and money. Marketers conduct this research to measure and compare people's activities, interests and opinions—what intrigues or fascinates them and what they believe or assume about the world around them. Lifestyle analysis tends to exclude demographic traits. Thus, a marketer such as Wills Sports might like to know more about men who play amateur cricket, with special focus on the heavy user who plays two or more games a week. A lifestyle survey could then be administered to this segment in order to identify other characteristics that would aid in product development and advertising planning aimed at them. Suppose we discovered that the majority of the men in the category exhibited the following lifestyle characteristics: play other amateur games, value the family, engage in social drinking, hold mostly liberal views and visit a place of worship regularly. This information would help us select media and write copy that would appeal to this segment. There are research firms that have taken lifestyle factors a step further by creating lifestyle profiles that collectively reflect a whole culture.

One example is the work of SRI International and their values and lifestyle systems (VALS). Advertisers could correlate these VALS groups with their clients' products and use this information to design ads and select media. Eventually, SRI discovered that the relationship between values and purchase was not very strong. So, they developed VALS2, which groups values and other psychological traits. VALS2 arranges psychographics groups in a rectangle. They are stacked vertically by resources and horizontally by self-attention (principle, status or action oriented). Resources include income, education, self-confidence, health, eagerness to buy and energy levels. A person's position along the resource and self-orientation axes determines which of eight classifications he falls into: Actualizer, Fulfilled, Achiever, Experiencer, Believer, Striver, Maker or Struggler. The members of each group hold different values and maintain different lifestyles. Obviously, knowing the psychographic orientation of consumers is a valuable asset to an advertiser in deciding at whom his message should be targeted.

To make the psychological study of advertisements effective and systematic, I will classify different ads under the following heads:

- Ads for the family
- Ads for men of the 1980s and 1990s
- Ads for the new man
- Ads for feminists
- Ads for children
- Ads with colour prejudice

Ads for the Family

In this category, I will cover ads that concentrate on family affairs and family members. These ads reflect the needs and values of Indian families and their slogans associate these with their products.

An ad for Samsung refrigerators has the tagline, *'Be a Freshetarian with Samsung Bio-Fresh Refrigerators'*. The body text is more convincing: *"Whether you're a vegetarian or a non-vegetarian, now it is time to become a Freshetarian."* The copywriter, who is

always in search of a striking new adjective or noun, often uses neologism as a device. A neologism, by extending the boundaries of the rules for the formation of words, widens the possibilities of expression. Both composition or compounding and derivation or affixation are used to form a neologism. Familiar recent examples are 'Kleenex' and 'Xerox', which began as invented trade names, but have quickly become everyday words in the language. In a different ad for Samsung refrigerators, a mother-in-law and daughter-in-law are shown arguing over buying fresh vegetables every day. After a few days, the mother-in-law is pleased because the daughter-in-law is putting fresh dishes on the dining table every day. But she does not know that the canny daughter-in-law has solved the problem by buying a Samsung Bio Fresh Refrigerator, which keeps food fresher, longer, and saves her a daily trip to the market.

When we suffer back pain, we need a balm for quick relief. One such brand of balm has a unique punchline: *'Trishun Rub: Sabka Rub Ek'*. To analyse the message, we should know the semantic description of language. In this ad, there is one word, 'rub', which makes all the difference because it has two interpretations: 'rub' as in a balm and 'rub', which is the Punjabi word for god. Semantically, such a term, with two or more unrelated meanings, would be known as a homonymy.

Phonological similarity heightens the effect of a message. So, lexical relations are the basis of a lot of word play and used in particular to achieve a humorous effect. The Pilsbury Flour Company once used homophony to promote its flour brand in its tagline: *'Everybody Kneads It'*. Synthesis of conception, economy of expression, the lyricism that contributes to retention in the memory—all these are the tools of a good poet, but also skills that are essential to good advertising.[7]

In the early years, vernacular advertising was a half-baked effort that lacked wider acceptance and professional skills. Ads were written mostly in English and copywriting in Hindi was a distant dream. But over the years, there has been a tremendous change, especially in Hindi advertising, which had never been considered market friendly. In the last ten years, there has emerged a great demand for bilingual copywriters. The Nirma jingle, "*Doodh si safedi,* Nirma *se aaye, rangeen kapda bhi khil-khil jaye, sabki pasand* Nirma", started the Hindi advertisements' success story. This was followed by some more original ads in Hindi: *'Surf Ki Kharidari Mein Hi Samajdhari', 'Dhoom Macha De, Rang Jama De'* (Pan Parag), and *'Daag Dhoondte Reh Jaoge'* (Surf Ultra). But now many companies are pressing copywriters to write ad scripts in Hindi for their products. Even multinational corporations have realised the importance of Hindi in reaching the larger chunk of India's population. Due to the rapid advancement of the electronic media, vernacular languages are becoming a popular medium for regional advertisements. I believe that Amul's advertising campaign has transformed the whole art of copywriting in India. It breaks the myth that English is essential to the success of an ad line. Amul has proved all ad gurus wrong. Its headlines are simple, short and memorable. However tense we are, they make us smile. And they are very topical as in the ad featured here, which takes off on the controversial incident in which Hollywood actor Richard Gere kissed Hindi film star Shilpa Shetty at a public HIV/AIDS function.

In another ad, Amul capitalises on the comeback of the famous Hindi film star, Madhuri Dixit, in the 2007 film, *Aaja*

Nachle (Let's Dance), the essence of which was music and dance. Everyone, including our Amul girl, is dancing and munching bread and butter on the dance floor, displaying the irresistible charm of Amul butter in the advertisement.

It shows the increasing popularity of Hindi that Thums Up's '*Taste the Thunder*' tagline was later developed as '*Toofani Thanda*'. Today, Hindi ads are equally saleable in the market. Recently, language mixing has become au courant, with many words using the Roman script in ads. Some popular headlines of this nature are:

- 'Na Piyoge to Pachtaoge' (New Tata Tea Gold)
- 'Tumse Hai Zindagi' (Samsung washing machine)
- 'Meethe Pal Phir Se' (Equal low calorie sweetener)
- 'Achhe Sehat ki Sanjeevani' (Hamdard's Rogan Badam Shirin)
- 'Zara Chakh ke Dekho' (Monginis)
- Fresh Ho Jao' (Limca)
- 'Mummy ka Magic Chalega Kya?' (Whirlpool)
- 'Promise Yahi, Weight Sahi' (HP Gas)
- 'The Josh Machine' (Ford Ikon)
- 'Chai Shai, Mast Ho Jaye' (Kurkure)

The understanding of both sense and reference is essential to proper understanding of the meaning of an ad. In non-technical language, the two are sometimes used interchangeably, but the difference between the two is considered crucial in semantics. The denotation of a word is the object or the objects that it refers to in the world's language. The denotation of the word, 'whale', is the whale found in the seas. The denotation of the word, 'elephant', is the animal you would expect to see in a jungle or in a zoo. The denotation of a word is, thus, the same thing as the referent of that word. But just as the meaning of the reference needs to be understood in relation to the meaning of the sense, the meaning of the denotation needs to be understood in relation to the meaning of the connotation. The 'connotation' of a word is the incidental meaning that we associate with the word from time to time. The putative qualities (qualities which are often supposed to be there) expressed by adjectives such as 'frail', 'sentimental', 'tender', 'likely to shed tears', 'kind' and 'compassionate' can, for example, be mentioned as some of the connotations of the word, 'woman'.

It may be pointed out here that though the denotation of a word usually remains the same, its connotation changes with the passage of time. In many cases, it also changes from one culture to another, and in some cases, it changes from one individual to another. Thus, the connotation of a word is unstable and, compared to its denotation, it is peripheral to its meaning.[8] 'Woman' has many avatars in the world of advertising. Recently, Horlicks introduced a variant aimed at women. The copy of the advertisement appeals to women by telling them why they also need Horlicks, a health drink once reserved for children. The ad puts the woman at the centre of all activities, showing her to be fit and successful in all the myriad chores she undertakes every day, whether in the home or at office. The ad clearly pitches the idea to women that everybody needs you and so your body needs Women's Horlicks.

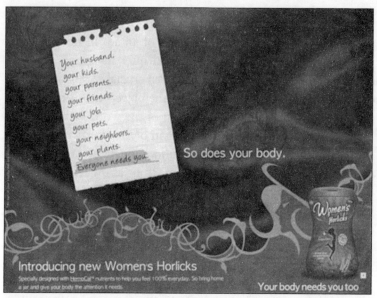

Copywriters collect considerable information before they start working on copy. They study research reports, such as psychographic studies and market trends, which are available from research organisations. In addition, copywriters collect first-hand information about the product, the prospects it is aimed at and their buying behaviour. They may even talk to people on the street and ask questions about the product. They may talk to retailers about the product and visit supermarkets to observe shoppers. Copywriters read magazines and listen to radio commercials. They want to know as many details as possible about the product and the prospects so as to prepare an ad message that is capable of stimulating the prospects to buy the advertised product. The copy must talk the language of the prospects—it must be so written that the audience will understand it easily. Al Ries and Jack Trout, the celebrated branding duo, write, *"If you want to catch a fish, you have to think like a fish. If you want to catch a consumer, you have to think like a consumer."*

In the ad for Trishun Rub (*'Sab Ka Rub Ek'*), the use of the word 'rub' is intended to produce lexical ambiguity because it means different things in English and Punjabi. In an ad for Godrej

Pentacool refrigerators, the tagline goes, *'Life Jum Jaye'*. If we have watched this commercial on television, we know that it is a wedding scene and everyone is busy because the bridegroom and his party are due to arrive any moment. The would-be mother-in-law is perplexed about how to chill drinks for so many people. Then the responsibility for serving cold drinks is shifted to film star Preity Zinta, a friend of the bride. Zinta brings in the Godrej Pentacool refrigerator and serves cold drinks to everyone's satisfaction and the wedding ceremony takes place in perfect amity. The tagline, *'Life Jum Jaye'*, conveys two messages. One, the Godrej Pentacool refrigerator sets *(jumana)* ice faster to serve chilled drinks. Two, Zinta sets *(jumana)* her friend's life by serving cold drinks to the bridegroom and his party. The body text also shows the beauty of the code mixing, which is a popular trend these days: "Godrej Pentacool brings you the latest in cooling technology—5 Side Funda, Fastest Thanda. Only the freezer of Preity's Godrej Pentacool cools from 5 sides, hence cools the fastest. The freezers in other refrigerators cool only from 4 sides. That's why Preity and her Godrej Pentacool are the coolest pair this summer."

Attitudes are a reflection of our values. Some ads are based on our heavy positive emotions. Advertisers cash in on our dreams and hopes and design messages to communicate a sense of joy or achievement. An advertisement for Bajaj Chetak says it like this: *'Apne Sapne ko Apne Paseene se Seenchna Padta Hai'* ('You Have to Water Your Dreams with Your Sweat'). The ad persuades a young man with good career prospects to realise his dreams by buying a scooter with his hard-earned money. The ad further says: *Jiyo to Imaan Se'*. It reinforces the prospect's image as an honest, hard-working man. Other positive emotional appeals involving price, prestige or exclusiveness are often employed in advertisements for fabrics and toiletries. If you are a successful man and do not want to miss out on anything in life, wear Raymond suits because they make you a *'Complete Man'*. Besides fabrics, Park

Avenue offers you a wide range of toiletries to nurture your personality:

'*Park Avenue: A Guide to the Well-Groomed Male*'

Advertising messages generally combine words and groups which can be interpreted denotatively as well as connotatively. Maruti Suzuki, India's largest car-selling company, advertised its new model, the Zen, thus: 'Maruti Zen: Just Add Zen to Your Life'. Here, the word, 'zen', is used with double meaning. Semantically, either you add a Maruti Zen car to your life or you add the Zen Buddhism way of life, which leads to a stress-free mind. It is also a comment on the technical collaboration between the Indian Maruti with the Japanese Suzuki, underlining the shared social and cultural values between the two countries, for Zen Buddhism travelled from India to Japan and is now practised widely there.

Advertising language, in which creativity is of the utmost importance, gives the copywriter almost unlimited scope for violating the rules and conventions of language. Just as the poet takes liberties with language in order to enrich his expression, the copywriter widens and deepens the potentialities of language in several ways.[9] The copywriter tries innovative ways and develops memorable and interesting ads. An ad for Gold Flake cigarettes, a premium ITC brand, sports the line: '*It's Honeydew Smooth*'. The ad makes an appeal with its mellow taste. The copywriter uses compounding as a device by combining two nouns to heighten the effect. The combining process of two separate words

(honey + dew), called compounding, is quite common in advertising language. There are many such formations: *'trendsetter'*, *'manpower'*, *'wrinklefree'*, *'waterproof'*, et cetera. Brand names consisting of noun + noun compounds are coming into fashion, often with a noun compounded with the manufacturer's trade name as in the case of Amulspray, Bisonbra, Milkmaid, Maidenform, Sunsilk and Warlord (toy gun); both together make up the trade name.[10]

There are marked phonological variations in the ad for Asian Paints, in which a neighbour admires Sudhir Babu's social achievements: "Sudhir Babu! *Naya ghar, nayi gaadi aur nayi 'missej'. Badhiya hai!*" The ad is designed in colloquial language. Two things are remarkable in the ad: First, the pronunciation of the word ('*missej*', instead of the usual 'missus') is not a standard one, and second, everything gets worn out with the passage of time except the house, which looks just the same as when it was new, thanks to the 'Time Proof Beauty' of Asian Paints.

Graphological violations are much more frequent in advertising language than in any other register. Both in the brand name and in the text of the advertisement, the copywriter can make almost unlimited use of spelling changes with the pronunciation remaining unchanged.[11] Sometimes, the copywriter exploits the phonological similarity between the word used in an

advertisement and the standard accepted word. The Ghari detergent company launches a new product, called Ghari 'Xpert' Dishwash Bar. In this ad, due to the phonological similarity, the word expert'/ eksp3:t/ is spelt as 'xpert', which does not change the pronunciation of the word. There are many ads in which the copywriter subtly employs such violations to design enchanting lines. There are many such instances in the Limca ads: 'tangi' for 'tangy', 'veri' for 'very', 'tasti' for 'tasty' and 'healthi' for 'healthy'. This trend in copywriting is not new; three decades ago, Thackersey fabrics used the line: *'Watch Everyone Make 'You' Turns'*. Today, Donear suitings has a line in its ad: *'Gifts 4 U'*.

Words and pictures work together to produce a creative concept. However, the idea behind a creative concept in advertising is usually expressed in some attention-getting and memorable phrases. Finding these 'magic words' is the responsibility of the copywriter, who searches for the right words to warm up the prospects' mood and soften resistance.[12] Versatility is a prime trait of copywriters. They can move from toilet paper to Taj Mahal and shift their writing style to match the product and the language of their target audience. Copywriters do not have a style of their own because the style they use has to match the message and the product. Like poets, copywriters spend hours, even days, creating ad copy. Copywriters use all the tools of a poet and exploit them to produce alluring copy, including rhyme, alliteration, rhythm, simile, metaphor, metonymy and parallelism. These literary techniques equip copywriters to enhance the memorability of headlines, subheads, slogans and taglines.

The most important way to create memorability is through repetition. Alliteration (the repetition of initial sounds) and rhyme are widely used literary devices in advertising language. Copywriters introduce rhythmic tones to create catchy slogans. The selection of beautiful words and sweet sounds multiply the 'saleability' of a product. A well-knit ad will draw everyone's attention and motivate them to buy a product. That is basically what advertising seeks to do. The following ads use some of these literary devices:

- 'Fun on the Run' (Maruti Alto)
- 'To Change The Way You Look'
  'Just Change The Way You Cook' (Samsung micro oven)
- 'Jal Jodo Jan Jodo, Jan Jodo Man Jodo' (Ministry of Water Resources)
- '5 Side Funda Fastest Thanda' (Godrej refrigerator)
- 'Young Ho Ya Old, Sabki Pasand Merrigold' (Merrigold margarine)
- 'Aaj Tak—Sabse Tez, Har Khabar Par Hamari Nazar' (Aaj Tak)
- 'Have a Break! Have a Kitkat' (Kitkat)
- 'Pet Me Pollution, Nityam Churna Hi Solution' (Zandu)

Besides deviations and figures of speech, copywriters use many other devices to create unforgettable messages. They accommodate numbers, symbols, signs and formulae in their ad copy. Manipulating numbers to give an exaggerated notion of the consumer's gain and a minimised version of his spending is one of the tricks of the trade. So, copywriters say, "Your safety costs just Rs 5 a day", rather than 'Rs 150 a month' or 'Rs 1,825 a year'. On the other hand, when it comes to gains, they say, "You will get interest of Rs 1,800 a year", rather than 'Rs 5 a day'. Zeroes have a mesmerising quality, which a smart copywriter exploits to sell.[13] The Bajaj Scooter ad picks up a similar theme and invites potential buyers with the '*Gaadi Bula Rahi Hain*' slogan, enticing them further with the message, '*Pay Just Rs. 999 and Drive Home a Bajaj Scooter*'. It is an impressive advertising as well as marketing strategy because very few people notice the asterisk that tails the Rs 999. It is never mentioned in the advertising copy that one has to pay regular monthly instalments at a pre-decided interest rate. So, at first sight, it succeeds in capturing the attention of people. The common man is thrilled to think that the scooter is so cheap. It is a psychological appeal to the consumer that there is no need to pay a large sum of money all at once. The ad also combines attractively the popular Hindi movie song with the eye-catching price of the scooter.

The magic of digits entices consumers in another ad, that of House Full, a home store, which appeals directly to customers through its attractive prices, which start from Rs 14,999. Zeros add to the impression of size. Rs 10,00,000 makes a heftier impression than Rs 1 million. And Rs 400.00 looks more significant than Rs 400. The Bajaj Pulsar claims record-breaking sales in its ad:

A Million Stars in the Sky
& 1,00,000 on the Road
The Bajaj Pulsar accelerates past the 1,00,000 landmark in record time

Besides the number game, the ad also relies on literary figures in the use of metonymy and similes. Metonymy (literally, a change of name) is effectively employed as the ad says, *'Millions in the Sky and 1,00,000 on the Road'*, without using the name of the motorbike. It is understood that the 1,00,000 stars on the road are meant to be Pulsar motorbikes. The simile (a comparison made between two objects of different kinds) comes in where the stars are compared with bikes.

Another ad for the Bajaj Pulsar satisfies the egoistic needs of its consumers. It targets a consumer who thinks that he is different or who has a desire to be something in life. It appeals to the acquired needs that we learn in response to our culture and environment. These may include needs for esteem, prestige, affection, power and learning. Here is one such ad:

In Just 18 Months, We've
Made 2,00,000 Celebrities

What the ad seeks to say here is:

"The unmatched combination of style, feature, power and mileage in the Pulsar motorbike makes every Pulsar owner a celebrity in his own right. So, while others make celebrities sell their bikes, we sell our bikes and make celebrities."

Some ad lines include mathematical signs to establish their product in the market. These signs could be anything, but they become effective and meaningful when they are used in context and according to where they are placed. All signs and symbols take a major part of their meaning from how and where they are placed—at the street corner, at a particular time in the history of the world. Our own bodies make and give off much of their meanings because of where they are and what they are doing 'in

place'. A person who is wearing no clothes on a public beach is a 'nude bather', whether legal or not. A person who is wearing no clothes in the privacy of his bathroom is simply a person going for a bath, not a 'nude bather'.[14]

When the Bajaj Caliber was given a five-star rating by a motor magazine, it boasted of this appreciation in one of its ads, saying:

***** *Rating: Hoodibaba!*

Until the stars (*) are placed in their right place, this sign only means a figure in the abstract. It becomes meaningful when it is associated with a real-world meaning. Now, in the ad, these five stars are represented as the epitome of quality and performance.

An ad for the TVS Victor uses another sign with a difference:

TVS Victor: More Smiles (per) Hour

The line is supposed to be scripted in terms of a scientific formula. Its Hindi version says, 'Meelon Chalti Muskan'.

In personification, inanimate objects and abstract notions are spoken of as having life and intelligence. This figure of speech is employed to suggest that even smiles can go miles. Or, in other words, one will smile longer because there is no need to fill the fuel tank as many times as with other motorbikes.

Two other ads make the following propositions:

Dettol: 'Be 100% Sure'

Anchor toothpaste: '100% Vegetarian'

In both ads, the percentage marks are used to emphasise the brand's unique selling proposition (USP). The numerical adjective (cardinal), 100, is effectively juxtaposed with the percentage mark to ensure the genuineness of the product. Dettol is a symbol

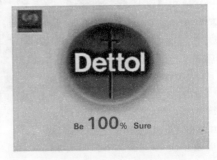

of good health and hygiene. So, its ad talks of purity as its USP. The second ad targets vegetarians. Brand Dettol tells you that using Dettol shows how much you love and care for your family. Brand Anchor holds forth a different appeal, targeted at a particular group that holds an aversion to non-vegetarian products. Perhaps the ad was designed when it was not customary for manufacturers to put the vegetarian mark on their products.

Ads for Men of the 1980s and 1990s

The sole aim of advertising is to sell a product. Through various appeals, advertising influences, rationally or emotionally, the buying behaviour of consumers. One product has many advertisements with different themes and set in various locales. For example, cola companies do vibrant advertising in the summer, but that does not stop them from advertising the rest of the year, too. Keeping potential buyers in view, many products are positioned through advertising in the market. These potential buyers are further classified on the basis of the products they use. There are many products that are exclusively targeted at men, women, children, single families, joint families, institutions, offices, et cetera. For example, McDonald's restaurants denote wholesome family treats.

In the world of advertising, positioning is the extremely simplified persona that the product represents in the mind of a typical consumer. It is the sum of those attributes normally ascribed to it by consumers—its standing, its quality, the type of people who use it, its strengths, its weaknesses, any other unusual or memorable characteristics it may possess, its price and the value it represents. Advertising is a powerful marketing tool—it creates and generates an image of the product in the mind of a consumer.

For more than two decades, men have been represented in ads as robust, uncompromising and emotionally unruffled. They are depicted as living for themselves in their own carefree world, answerable to none. They are shown carrying the unnecessary burden of their manly image. Marlboro has become the world's most successful cigarette thanks to the exciting, masculine, cowboy world that its ads depict, which has been equally effective all over the world, regardless of culture. Marlboro has identified its masculine cowboy environment and stuck to it through thick and thin. The essential gambit—positioning a cigarette as masculine by featuring a particularly masculine environment—is not new, but Marlboro was more successful than most in pulling it off.

Another cigarette brand, Red & White, uses a sexy, well-built man as the hero in its ads. The Red & White hero is always rescuing someone from danger in the cigarette's ads. Its tagline says, '*Hum Red & White Peene Walon Ki Baat Hi Kuchh Aur Hai*'.

Other examples of macho ads are those for Wills Filter ('*Made for Each Other*'), MRF Tyres ('*Muscle Man*'), Lifebuoy ('*Tandurusti Ki Raksha Karta Hai Lifebuoy*') and Enfield Bullet ('*Who Says Tough Guys Don't Dance*'). Cigarettes and beer have much in common with them, but they also have an extra dimension that distinguishes them from the rest. Cigarettes and beer define the type of person you are and the personality you want to present to the world.[15] In the global market, Armagnac, a distinctive brandy made in Gascony in Southwest France, is positioned as an exclusive brandy.

ARMAGNAC
Pass It On
France's Oldest Brandy
Not the Best Known, but Known by the Best

The ad highlights two things: First, that Armagnac is the oldest brandy of France, and second, that it appeals to people who like to be one-up on others in their choice of drinks in order to demonstrate prestige and knowledge. Again, the ad elevates the pride and status of a man.

Other positive emotional appeals involving the prestige and exclusiveness of men are often used in advertisements for suitings.

Advertisements for suitings by companies such as Raymond, Digjam and Dinesh employ emotional ploys. *'Suitings for the Connoisseur'*, a Digjam ad campaign, appeals to individuals who are experts in matters of taste and choice of clothing. Digjam also used well-known cricketer Nawab Mansoor Ali Khan Pataudi in its ads. The Vimal ad featured newsmakers to promote 'the Finest Suitings for Performance in the Age Group of 31-Plus'. Cricketer Sachin Tendulkar flaunts his 'Visa Power' and tells us to *'Go and Get It'*. In another ad, Tendulkar's shot hits the window of a Pepsi truck, but he still gets his bottle of Pepsi. So, men and their machismo have dominated the advertising business for a very long time. But now that's slowly changing, with the new man replacing the Macho Man.

Ads for the New Man

Men, especially in urban India, are no longer living in an insulated ethos. With the opening up of the economy, a gamut of new professions has emerged and lifestyles have changed considerably. As an increasing number of Indians travel abroad, the acquiring does not stop at the latest Hugo cologne, it includes attitudes and mindsets, too. While globalisation has played its part, the crucial cause of the metamorphosis of the Indian man is the Indian woman. She is a driving force in his life today. The Grasim suitings  television commercial targets the girlfriend, rather than the man who will wear the suit. The Indian man is being increasingly defined by what his woman expects of him. As women step out of their homes and into boardrooms, they are having a large say in decision-making.

Advertising reflects this transition. Ads, even for conventionally male products, are now scripted keeping women also in mind. "It is becoming essential to appeal to a woman's sensibilities as she may often have the final say," says well-known ad-maker Prahlad Kakkar. Or at least, she will influence the decision because, usually, the man is spending generously to impress her.

Ever wondered what makes Sachin Tendulkar smile? Bludgeoning Shoaib Akhtar for a six? Wrong. Donning a chef's hat and cooking for his friends. While conceptualising a television commercial for a two-wheeler, Kakkar put this question to the batting genius and the prompt reply was, "Spending time with friends and family." So, Tendulkar is seen on TV cooking a meal for his friends, not hitting out at fast bowlers, and cleaning his motorbike, instead of zooming around on it.[16]

There is noticeable change in the behavioural patterns of young Indian men. A recent study conducted by the advertising agency, Rediffusion DYR, indicates that the hitherto dogmatic, self-centred young Indian man has changed. Whether he plays football with his wife and children in the rain or offers his wife a helping hand in washing clothes (Samsung) or repairs his house to surprise his family (Asian Paints), he is more sensitive and caring

than his earlier avatar. He achieves many things in life and shares his life with his family and friends. The Asian Paints Royale commercial, in which Hindi film actor Akshaye Khanna puts up a sepia family photograph on a freshly painted wall illustrates the attempt at 'building bridges with the past'. Even as they stride rapidly towards being tech-savvy, men still wish to hold on to their roots and want to be considered an integral part of Indian culture.

Whether it is the Pepsi commercial, in which film star Saif Ali Khan presumes the bevy of beauties is vying for him, only to learn that they want only his bottle of Pepsi, or the Akai Sure Shot ad, in which the man plummets into a gutter just as he is about to speak to a gorgeous woman, "it is the ultimate dig at the macho male", says Alyque Padamsee. "The Indian man is finally beginning to laugh at himself".[17]

Some feel advertising is trying too hard to make up for its earlier sexist leanings, and often going over the top in the effort. Piyush Pandey, executive chairperson and national creative director, O&M, India's South Asia, who has many awards to his credit, says that advertising is guilty of projecting Indian men as soppy. "The Indian male believes in the equality of the sexes and not taking a woman for granted. But a man listening to the sound of a baby as he puts his ear to the stomach of a pregnant woman is an instance of trying too hard," he says. "Earlier he was excessively macho, now he is too mushy".[18]

The first signs of this change came in the early

Feels like heaven
doesn't is
Feels like Raymonds

1990s with the first of Raymond's 'Complete Man' series of ads, in which the spotlight was turned from biceps to sensitivity. The earlier campaigns focused on grooming and dressing better. Later, the focus shifted to portraying the man as establishing emotional connections with his friends, his woman and now his baby, but refrained from featuring glamorous women revealing plenty of skin. Women are dressing and looking sexier, but "a woman doesn't mean sex", says Nabankur Gupta, group president, Raymond.[19]

The change in the Indian man, says Kakkar, is only superficial. "There are two kinds of men: a men's man and a ladies' man. He is boorish and loud when he is with his buddies, and sensitive and caring when he wants to impress women."

Superficial or not, the Indian man has changed. Psychiatrist Harish Shetty says the Indian man has always been sensitive, only "soft often meant gay".[20] Now, he is more visible because the emotional ambience of many families has evolved and men and women often switch roles in the household.

Ads for Feminists

There is a new kind of woman on television and she is all the things Mummy said you should never grow up to be. She's selfish, actively aggressive and—the biggest sin in Mummy's book—really doesn't know how a lady should behave around men. Even Lalitaji, TV's once super-aggressive female icon, would have dropped her shopping bag in shock.[21]

Few years back, two companies launched their summer apparel campaigns. One was Levi's low-waist jeans ('Low Rise Jeans, Dangerously Low'). The other was Lovable inner wear ('Keeps You Cool'). The ads for these two products were packed with sensuous visuals and no words. The message was conveyed through the sensual picturisation of young, sexy, teenage girls in the scanty clothes they were advertising, bursting with oomph and energy. While one would not like to get into issues of ethics and morality, the assault on decency cannot be denied.

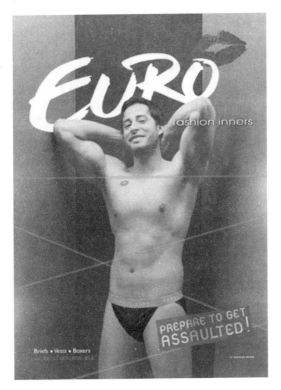

The new Indian woman in advertising is thus brave, confident and outrageous to the extent of shamelessness. In the Rupa underwear TV advertisement, the male model (Zulfi Syed) has been subjected to female molestation, going by the lipstick marks on his bare body, when he enters a women's restroom by mistake. The ad carries a bold tagline: *'Prepare to Get Assaulted'*. It indicates that men who wear Rupa inner wear should be prepared for the effect it has on women.

Ads in the 1980s portrayed women as homemakers for their macho men. At the end of the 1990s arrived the sensitive, complete man, but women were still sex symbols. Now, the ad world is treading where it did not dare to tread before, in creating sexist, abusive, insensitive, hormone-driven, chauvinist women. We see this woman at her best in the Sansui ad, where she seduces a man while his wife is in another room. Her jeans may be distressed and the bounce in her hair carefully controlled, but we cannot say the same about her hormones. There is so much oestrogen floating around her that we could produce telly tube babies. In the VIP ad, similarly, two young girls are shown spying on a boy from their balcony with a pair of binoculars. The unsuspecting boy is exercising at home, wearing nothing but his briefs.

The Femina commercial has a bride who, far from being blushing and coy on the marital bed, wrests sexual supremacy from her new husband to become the *'ad world's first bride on top'*. Also showing on TV is a female doctor who evidently does a very good job of eyeing her patient's boyfriend, who is strolling unsuspectingly in the waiting room (*'Men in Parx, Girlfriends Beware'*).

"The Feast ice cream ad, in which the 'f' word was used with a female association for the first time in India, and the Close-Up spot, in which John Abraham was kissed by a woman in power, can be said to have started the trend," says adman Shivjeet Khullar. "And though they were ahead of their times and rejected at the time, what they did do was break

new ground." Khullar predicts that with the recall value the ads establish, "in the coming years, you are going to see a lot more of these 'femnas' on TV".

Anup Chitnis, executive creative director, O&M, refers to it as a "very surprising trend". He says, "The woman was traditionally the aggressive protagonist in ads where the consumers were women because they liked to see themselves as winners." This is what marketing professionals call 'aspirational advertising'. But adds Chitnis, "What you're seeing now is the female as the protagonist in ads where the consumer is traditionally a man".[22] We can reach the reasonable conclusion then that men, the target audience for these ads, seem to find female domination acceptable. Or, at least, this is what the advertisers wish to show us.

Freddie Birdy, co-founder, Shop, speaks for his clan when he hails it as a sign of the times. "For years, men have called the shots and they know it. Now, women have changed," he says. "They are now more confident about their sexuality and ready to express it. Not in a girlie, kitty party, 20 women giggling together type of way, but in bars and other social situations. Advertising is reflecting this, albeit in an exaggerated way",[23] says Birdy.

Such advertising shows that sexuality is integral to consumerist trends in which the fastest objects to sell are those concerning the body. The message of women's empowerment, as far as audiences go, is as suspicious as advertisers say it is sublime. Former minister for information and broadcasting Sushma Swaraj's objection, tellingly, was not because a chained John Abraham was being kissed by his female jailor in  the Close-Up ad, but because she didn't think a kiss should be shown on TV. The current advertising trend is not being rejected totally by society because feedback and market research suggest that audiences do identify with the changing gender equations at some level.

While agreeing that aggressive women are the Indian ad world's newest creations, Shantanu Kumar, supervisor, account planning, Enterprise Nexus, the agency that created the 'bride on top' ad for Femina, says, "It would be correct to call it a general trend as most of these ads belong to product categories that make an attitude statement, rather than mass product categories, which would not be quite so dramatic and would strike a balance".[24] It is important to make a distinction between the two, he adds. He may be right, but who will try to explain this to Mummy?

Top of the World: The Woman Wrests Power in the 'Bride on Top' Femina Ad

| A newly married couple is ushered into their room on their wedding night. The door is bolted from outside amid sniggers and chuckles. | The bride and groom make their way to the well-decorated bed and sit on the edge, sharing an uncomfortable silence. |

| The groom sneaks a peak at his new wife and squirms in his seat, discomfited. | The woman sees his painfully awkward expression. Amused, she smiles to herself. |

Slowly, she gets up and inches her way towards him and makes the first move. Reaching out, she removes his head gear.

She climbs on the bed and gives his chest a nudge. Our man, numb with shock, stares

She removes her head gear and lets her hair fall around her face.

The Femina super appears on the screen: 'Generation W'.

Source: www.afaqs.com.

Ads for Children

"Sell them their dreams. People, especially kids, don't buy things to have things. They buy hope. Sell them this hope and you won't have to worry about your sales." This celebratory song of a society high on materialism at a salespersons' conference sums up the reality of contemporary urban life. It turns adolescents into a significant consumer segment—individuals who are not dependent on their parents, but who have an increasing urge to flaunt everything from mobile phones to designer clothes.

Advertising promotes and shapes the buying behaviour of children and traps them with enticing language and the right appeals. On the basis of market research on the psychological needs of children, advertisers frame advertisements with one big selling idea to beguile them to possess an item or a product. Children are defining themselves by what they possess. *'I buy, therefore I am'* has become the mantra for today's teens. It is a recurrent trend that is widely prevalent through Indian urban society. For children, 'possessions' mean branded products that spell status and popularity. Gone are the days of cheap canvas shoes and home-sewn frilly frocks. Girls now want Mango T-shirts and designer jeans. Boys who were earlier brought up to take pride in ink-stained shirts and scuffed shoes now worry about what gel works best in their hair and what model of mobile phones they should sport. Their list of 'must-haves' reads like the catalogue of a sophisticated mall: trendy clothes, watches, cosmetics, accessories, shoes, mobile phones, CDs, music systems, smart computers and laptops, sports gear, hair dryers and umpteen other gizmos—all the fancy paraphernalia of the 'with it' lifestyle. The latest 'necessity' is add-on credit cards over and above a fat weekly allowance for trips to hangout joints and beauty salons.

Many parents are worried that consumerism may be trapping their children into a self-centred way of life. However, Susan Visvanathan, sociologist at Delhi's Jawaharlal Nehru University, argues that consumerism is part of the grammar of a globalised capitalist society. "Children who coerce parents into more goodies are only victims of a system," she says. "The system does not believe in martyrs, only in survivors. Survival seems to mean an ability to enjoy without looking at the conditions of the majority," she explains.[25]

Role models have also changed. Mahatma Gandhi, Jesus Christ and Mother Teresa are no longer the personalities children idolise. Their icons and role models are the glitzy pop artists and film stars they see in TV programmes, films and advertisements. Youngsters tend to take the materialism expounded in ads as the gospel truth. Advertisers target children as surrogates to advertise 'adult' goods such as cars and even credit cards. LG Electronics, for example, uses children in the ads for its TVs and refrigerators.

Manufacturers know they can win the approval of parents for their brands by promotions in schools. In an interview to *Kidscyclopedia*, a Net magazine, Reebok's managing director, Subhinder Singh Prem, says their 'Net Practice with Rahul Dravid' campaign 2003 was a big hit.[26] The campaign offer was a chance to join a cricket camp with cricketer Rahul Dravid on buying Reebok goods worth Rs 1,500 or more. Advertisers take advantage of the fact that children are the most important and dominating members in every family today. As per advertising strategy, kids are the most easily wooed targets in a family and what they want is seldom denied.

"Wooing kids means wooing the entire family because children drive the spending decisions," says Amit Burman, vice chairman, Dabur India.[27]

Children, however, are a tough audience to please. Research suggests that simple language registers quickly with children. They tend to reject miscast actors, messages lost in too many words and images that fail to grab them in the opening seconds. By seven years of age, most children understand what advertisers are trying to achieve, and by ten years, they become critical. For all age groups, television advertising is a part of entertainment, so TV is an infallible advertising medium.

Packaging means a lot to children. "The right mix of entertainment, humour and a general dose of parental approval has the desired effect on children," says Kaurendra Mathur, director of Montage Advertising.[28] But most important of all is the brand positioning or the motivating message that the brand intends to convey and how it differs from its competitors. Children need to be lured at all levels to get them to try a brand and stick to it. Restaurant chains such as Pizza Hut and McDonald's have been quick to catch on to the ways of attracting children. They offer birthday party packages, complete with return gifts and decorations, to make sure that the restaurants register in children's minds as pleasure zones. Boomer Bubble Gum, which commands an almost 55 per cent share of the chewing gum market, followed a similar strategy. The brand is synonymous with its superhero, Boomer Man, who has fantasy power and is a proven winner with children. Its jingle, *'Boom, Boom, Boomer'*, has spontaneous recall, too. It is one booming formula.

Ads with Colour Prejudice

It would be laughable if it was not so pathetic. Barely have we finished celebrating the life of Kalpana Chawla as an Indian woman who broke through all barriers, including those in space, when there comes the argument over whether women's lib should come in light tones or dark. The issue reached Parliament when the All-India Democratic Women's Association sent letters in protest against some commercials on TV deemed offensive, following which the Ministry of Information and Broadcasting sent notices to a few television channels to take the ads off air. A handful · of commercials were deemed objectionable, including those of ICICI, Jockey underwear, Kamasutra condoms and Bacardi Breezer. But directly in the line of fire was the beauty industry's most uncomfortable success story—fairness creams, a segment whose annual market size in India is estimated at Rs 650 crore. Singled out were Hindustan Unilever Ltd's (HUL's) Fair & Lovely commercials. One of these ads begins with a girl voicing a commentary for a cricket

match being played in her street. In the next shot, her sister hands her a tube of Fair & Lovely and the street commentator turns into a professional commentator. The ad ends on a note of promise: *'Fair & Lovely, Zindagi Roshan Kare'*. The ad says indirectly that in order to achieve your ambitions in life, you must have a fair complexion.

Even as feminists called the ads 'humiliating and ludicrous', the offending brand, Fair & Lovely, quietly put out a press release announcing the launch of the Foundation for the Economic Empowerment of Women, with the backing of 'prominent women organisations and achievers' such as the renowned dancer, Mallika Sarabhai, and the former vice-chancellor of the University of Mumbai, Dr Snehlata Deshmukh. In all fairness though, isn't there a dichotomy in promoting economic empowerment and simultaneously putting out ads that show dark women to be inferior?

Another ad for Fair & Lovely has the father of a girl saying, "*Kaash mera ladka hota* (If only I had a son)", after which snub, his daughter uses the fairness cream, becomes fair (and, therefore, pretty) and lands the coveted job of, no, not a rocket scientist, but an air hostess. This unnecessary glorification of fair skin not only promotes false notions of beauty based on skin tones, it is also highly insulting to worldwide struggles against colour discrimination. Another ad shows a father who is worried that a prospective bridegroom will reject his daughter just as he has several other girls for the 'sin' of being dark. Again, Fair & Lovely steps in with the solution. Going by the matrimonial ads in the classified columns of newspapers, it would seem that a fair complexion is the most important definer of beauty in India. With such an attitude firmly entrenched in the minds of millions of people, the fairness products industry will never see dark days.

In all its ads, Fair & Lovely turns ordinary girls into whatever they want to be in life. In a recent ad, a girl is disappointed to find very few people in a theatre to watch her show. The director tells her, "*Agar koi* film star stage *pe hota na, hamara* theatre *bhi* house full *hota* (If there had been a film star on the stage, our theatre would also have run house full)." Then comes the saviour in the form of Fair & Lovely. The ad shows that the girl is determined to make it big as an actor and she uses the product and becomes fair and beautiful. Following the change in her appearance, she not only gets a lead role in a film, but also becomes a famous film star. The ad ends with the message: "*Khoobsoorati Hai Shakti. Fair & Lovely*".

According to statistics, fairness creams worth Rs 3,36,000 crore are sold in Asia.[29] This despite unanimous expert opinion that no fairness cream can make you any fairer than you were at birth. All it can do is reverse the damage done by unprotected

exposure to sun through ingredients like hydroquinore, which prevent the formation of melanin-producing cells and kill existing ones to make the skin tone lighter. Despite suspicions about the actual benefits of these creams, manufacturers and advertisers have shown that the products pass technical requirements.

In a country where even the gods supposedly lament their dark complexion—Krishna sings plaintively, "Radha *kyun gori, main kyun kala* (Why is Radha so fair when I'm dark)?"—a skin deficient in melanin, the pigment that determines the skin's colour, is sought after most eagerly.[30] It is embarrassing that our society is still preoccupied with 'whiteness'. How long can we judge a woman's merit on the false parameter of skin colour? Perhaps we need to become more aware and better educated. But 'dark' models and film stars such as Madhu Sapre, Kajol and Bipasha Basu have proved that they are the 'white' hopes of the glamour world.

Male Grooming

It is becoming an all-beautiful world. If you thought women are the only ones being pampered by the cosmetics companies for that perfect makeover, take a look around. In June 2005, an advertisement appeared on most TV channels which showed a teenaged boy slinking into a girls' hostel to steal a fairness cream. Just escaping being caught, he is chided by his friend, who advises him to get his own fairness cream, meant for men. The young man

procures such a cream, uses it and turns out 'fair and handsome'. In 2005, with the launch of Fair and Handsome, Emami became the first company in India to launch an 'only for men' fairness cream. Emami collaborated with Activor Corp. of the US and several herbalists and dermatologists in India to create the product. Because Fair and Handsome was a category creator, heavy promotion

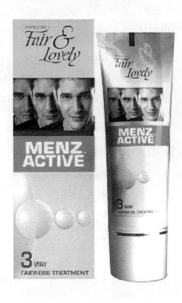

supported its launch. The theme of the brand's advertisements brought out the fact that a large number of men used women's fairness creams. The new customers of the beauty industry are men and various skincare brands, both national and international, are increasingly targeting them with their products. Within India, we have Emami's Fair and Handsome, HUL's Menz Active and Kaya Skin Clinics wooing men with their products and services.

Men are paying more attention to themselves than ever before. And marketers are happy to give them everything they want—even fairness creams. Clearly, brands want to reach their target in the most effective way. When Nivea launched its men's fairness product, Nivea for Men, it deliberately didn't term it a fairness cream. Shoma Ghosh of Nivea India explains, "The word 'fairness' is attached to women and men don't associate with it. Hence, we call it a skin whitening cream, thereby creating a new category."

By 2010, the male-grooming market could well cross the Rs 1,200 crore mark, with men spending more time in front of the mirror, more players vying for a share of this market, and the semi-urban male population also becoming part of this revolution.[31]

Notes

1. Valladares, June A., 2000. *The Craft of Copywriting*. New Delhi: Response Books, p. 46.

2. Ibid., p. 107.

3. Wells, William, John Burnett and Sandra Moriarty, 2003. *Advertising: Principles and Practice*. New Delhi: Pearson Education Inc., p. 99.

4. Ibid., p. 109.

5. Ibid., p. 111.

6. Tandon, Tina, 2002. 'Utterly, Butterly, Forever', in *Brand Equity*, supplement of *The Economic Times*. Feb 13, pp. 1–3.

7. Valladares, June A, 2000. *The Craft of Copywriting*. New Delhi: Response Books, p. 30.

8. Thakur, D., 1999. *Semantics*. Patna: Bharti Bhawan, pp. 14–5

9. Pandya, Indubala H., 1977. *English Language in Advertising*. Delhi: Ajanta Publication, pp. 14–5.

10. Ibid., p. 13.

11. Ibid., p. 12.

12. Wells, William, John Burnett and Sandra Moriarty, 2003. *Advertising: Principles and Practice*. New Delhi: Pearson Education Inc., p. 333.

13. Thomas, Sunny, 1997. *Writing for the Media*. New Delhi: Vision Books Pvt. Ltd., pp. 106–7.

14. Scollon, Ron, and Suzie Scollon, 2003. *Discourse in Place: Language in the Material World*. London: Routledge, Taylor & Francis Group, p. 2.

15. Harrison, Tony, 1987. *A Handbook of Advertising Technique*. London: Kogan Page Ltd., p. 24.

16. Doshi, Anjali, 2003. 'Tender is the Knight', in *India Today*. December 22, pp. 61–2.

17. Ibid.
18. Ibid.
19. Ibid.
20. Ibid.
21. Gahlaut, Kanika, 2002. 'Out of the Box', in *India Today*. November 25, pp. 72–3.
22. Ibid.
23. Ibid.
24. Ibid.
25. Vasudev, Shefalee, 2002. 'Material Children', in *India Today*. October 28, pp. 61–3.
26. Ibid.
27. Ibid.
28. Ibid.
29. Gahlaut, Kanika, 2003. 'White Lies', in *India Today*. March 31, p. 73.
30. Sinha, Suchi, 2000. 'Fair & Glowing', in *India Today*. December 4.
31. Nair, Sapna, 2007. 'A Fair Share of Attention', in *The Brand Reporter*. October 16–31, p. 14.

Five

Discourse Analysis of Advertising Language

You are judged by the way you speak:

An old sage once sat meditating under a banyan tree. He was blind. A man came up and said, "Hey, old man, did you hear anyone pass this way?" The sage replied, "No, my good man, I did not hear anyone."

After a while, another man went up to the old sage and asked, "Old man, did you hear anyone go this way?" The sage replied, "Oh yes, a man went by just now and he asked the same question." The man went away.

After some time, a third man came and asked, "Noble sir, did you hear anyone pass this way?"

The old sage replied, "Yes, Your Majesty. A soldier went first and then your chief minister. Both of them asked the same question."

The man was surprised and asked, "Good sir, how do you know that I am a king and that the other two were a soldier and a chief minister?

The sage answered, "Your Majesty, I knew them by their manner of speaking. The first man spoke very rudely. The second man was a little more polite, but Your Majesty was the most polite."

Think Inc./P. Batra

The study of discourse is the study of language independent of the notion of sentences. This usually involves studying longer (spoken and written) texts, but, above all, it involves examining the relationship between a text and the situation in which it occurs. So, even a short notice saying *'No Bicycles'* can be studied as discourse. Michael McCarthy suggests that a discourse analyst would be interested in the following questions about the notice:

- Who wrote the notice and to whom is it addressed (as, for example, an authority figure addressing the general public. This might explain what appears to be a rather abrupt, elliptical imperative: *"Don't ride/park your bicycle here!"*).
- How do we know what it means? In fact, in the situation from which it was taken (the window of a bicycle hire shop), it meant, "We have no more bicycles left to hire out." The notice was displayed during the high season for bicycle hires, and the most plausible interpretation was that the shop was informing potential customers that it had run out of bicycles. So, the grammar was not an imperative, but a statement. What factors enable us to interpret this? They are not 'in' the text, but an interpretation based on the text in its context.[1]

The preceding chapter concentrated on the psychological interpretation of meaning in advertising language. However, there are other aspects of meaning that are not derived solely from the meanings of the words used in phrases and sentences. In everyday conversation, when we come across bits of language, we normally try to understand not only what the words mean, but what the writer or speaker of those words intends to convey. The study of intended speaker meaning is a significant element in discourse analysis. As language users, when we make sense of what we read in texts, understand what speakers mean despite what they say, recognise connected as opposed to jumbled or incoherent discourse, and successfully take part in that complex activity called conversation, we are undertaking what is known as discourse analysis.

In order to interpret discourse in advertisements, we look into the proper representation of the form and structure used in advertising language. But as language users, we have a better understanding of language and its correct and incorrect forms and structure; so, when we analyse discourse strategies in ads, we go beyond the limitations of proper form and structure in language. We can read notices like 'No Pass, No Entry' on the main entrance of a sports stadium and understand that a conditional relationship exists between the two phrases. There are many such texts that we encounter regularly, which tend to break a number of language rules. Despite lapses, we understand what is conveyed on a notice board.

I once saw a notice drawing attention to a roadside garment sale: 'Fix Rate Rs 100 Any Item'. Despite the grammatical errors in the statement, we understand what the salesman wants to convey. The form of the message is not accurate. 'Fix' (the noun form) is used instead of 'Fixed' (the adjective form) unintentionally. Nevertheless, I did not experience any problem in arriving at a reasonable interpretation of what the salesman intended to convey. It is this effort to interpret, and how we accomplish it, that is the key element that the study of discourse investigates.

While processing written texts, we make the distinction between text features and discourse features. Text features, in J.D.A. Widdowson's view, are concerned mainly with propositional development, while discourse features are related to illocutionary development. Propositional development helps the author achieve cohesion, that is, 'the contextual appropriacy of linguistic forms—sentences and parts of sentences'. Cohesion can be described in terms of the syntactic and semantic links between sentences and their parts and these are usually signalled overtly.

In normal discourse, sentences do not in themselves express independent propositions—they acquire value in relation to other sentences. Successful communication presupposes the recognition of this relationship. Various procedures of cohesion are employed in written texts, of which the following have a high frequency: patterns of anaphora and cataphora, lexical and grammatical substitution, ellipsis, repetition and equivalence. These devices serve as propositional links and we recognise them because of our knowledge of certain facts about the English language.

Discourse features are not necessarily dependent on such overt cohesive linguistic signals. These acts are related to the illocutionary acts that the propositions are used to perform and these features reveal that illocutionary acts are not bound by language. They have more to do with logic than language. Thus, we recognise illocutionary acts such as defining, classifying, describing, explaining, inferring, identifying, and so on. In interpreting a written text, tracing the illocutionary development is as crucial for successful communication as working out the propositional development. The illocutionary value of propositions has to be inferred by recognising the cohesive links that exist between them. The way propositions are expressed and arranged sequentially has an effect on what they count as in terms of illocutionary value. Coherence is directly related to the appropriate illocutionary value of the propositions in a given piece of discourse. A sequence of illocutionary acts that is familiar, normal and easy to process is said to be coherent.

We know that texts must have a certain structure which depends on factors quite different from those required in the structure of a single sentence. Some of these factors are described in terms of cohesion. The text of the following advertisement could be assessed on the basis of its cohesive ties within the text:

IDBI Suvidha Fixed Deposits with higher return put back smiles in your life.

Suvidha offers you two options (i) Cumulative (ii) Non-cumulative. The deposits can be for a period of 1 to 5 years.

So, bid goodbye to your worries and say Hello to Happiness with IDBI Suvidha Fixed Deposits.

Bonding through Safety & Security.

In this advertisement, connections are created through the use of nouns which we assume are used to maintain reference to the same people and things: 'Suvidha', 'Fixed Deposits', 'Smiles', 'Happiness', 'Safety', 'Security'. These terms represent a common semantic link and reinforce the single theme that this investment is truly a *suvidha* (convenience) in all respects. To make the proposition more effective, two antonyms are used intelligently in the text: Bid 'goodbye' to your 'worries' and say 'hello' to 'happiness'.

We find a different piece of discourse in the ad for the Hyundai Santro car. The text in the ad is immensely persuasive and tells the man of the house how a 'special wife' (the specialities are defined in the text) deserves a car like the Hyundai Santro. The print ad has a long, but well-crafted, text.

Here the text is quite simple in structure and the proposition is self-explanatory. All the statements made here have the illocutionary value of an invocation calling upon a husband to take suitable action. The ad is persuading the husband (mentioned nowhere in the ad) to gift (not buy) a Santro car to his wife, who's special in so many ways. With its heavy emotional overtones, the complete discourse, with its eulogy to 'Mrs Special', is addressed to 'Mr Husband'. The discourse concludes with the message: If your wife is special, why not make her feel so by giving her something equally special, like a Hyundai Santro? The ad cashes in on the intimate sentiments of a husband and convinces him to buy

Your Wife

There's something special about her.

In the way she looks at you.

In the way she smiles.

In the way she squeezes your hand

when you are feeling low.

In the way she makes your house

feel like a home.

There's something special

in the way she says

her father is the best man in her life,

with a twinkle that tells you

he's not the only one.

There's something special

in the way she just fits into your life.

You know she's special.

Gift her something that'll make her feel so.

Santro Zip Plus
Automatic

The Simplest Car to Drive

his wife a new car. The whole text is cohesive and phrases such as 'in the way' are repeated to highlight the pronoun, 'she'. There is also a connector, 'there's', which marks the relationship of what follows to what went before by talking of the 'special qualities' of the wife in the entire ad. The tagline says, *'The Simplest Car to Drive'*. This is an indirect speech act in that it does not tell you directly to buy the Hyundai Santro, but that you should buy it because it makes driving so simple that your special wife will have a smooth ride in it.

Another key concept in discourse analysis is coherence, which exists not in language, but in people. It is people who 'make sense' of what they hear and read. They try to arrive at an interpretation that is in line with their experience of the world. This process is not restricted to trying to understand odd texts. In one way or another, it seems to be involved in our interpretation of all discourse. It is certainly present in the interpretation of casual conversation. We are continually taking part in conversational interactions in which a great deal of what is meant is not actually present in what is said. Perhaps, it is the ease with which we ordinarily anticipate each other's intentions that makes this whole complex process seem so unremarkable. Here is a good example adapted from Widdowson:

Nancy: That's the telephone
Ron: I'm in the bath
Nancy: O.K.

There are certainly no cohesive ties within this fragment of discourse, but people still manage to make sense of what is happening. They do use the information contained in the sentences, but there must be something else involved in the interpretation. It has been suggested that exchanges of this type are best understood in terms of the conventional actions by the speakers in such interactions. In this example, it is clear that language users must have a lot of knowledge of how conversational interaction works, all of which is not simply linguistic knowledge.

Ron Scollon and Suzie Scollon, in their book, *Discourse in Place: Language in the Material World*, talk of geosemiotics, the study of the social meaning of the material placement of signs and discourses and of all actions in the material world. Everywhere about us in our everyday world, we see the discourses which shape, manage, entice and control our actions. Instrumental to the process of shaping these discourses are the objects by which we index our own positions and identities in the world. The traffic light at a busy intersection not only narrowly manages the flow of automobiles through the intersection, it also indexes the municipal regulatory powers and apparatus which have placed the traffic light there and which maintain its functioning. Furthermore, as we approach the light and make our choices about stopping or driving through it, we index ourselves with respect to those regulatory powers and that municipal power apparatus. Mostly, of course, we index ourselves as law-abiding citizens by stopping when instructed to do so.

All signs, whether they are icons or symbols, are also indexes. This is because all signs must be located in the material world in order to exist. Information and knowledge must be presented by a system of signs, such as icons, symbols and indexes; information and knowledge cannot have any independent existence. The familiar Stop sign on a street corner is a symbol in several ways. The letters 'S', 'T', 'O' and 'P' symbolise the English word 'Stop', which itself symbolises the meaning, *'Progress No Further'*. It also symbolises this meaning through the conventional use of a red colour on a hexagonal background. Until it is placed in the world, this sign only means to stop in the abstract. On the sign painter's bench, it does not mean that he should stop painting. It only means that a car should stop when it is placed physically in the world in a place such as a street. This shift from abstract meaning potential to actual, real-world meaning is the property of 'indexicality'. Indexes have meaning in the real material and social world in which we live. So, indexicality is a property of the context dependency of signs, especially language, and hence, the study of those aspects of meaning which depend on the placement of the sign in the material world.

The Scollons discuss the 'in place' meanings of signs and discourses and the meanings of our actions in and among those discourses in place. A municipal ordinance prohibiting nude bathing or driving above a certain speed limit is an outcome of a complex and lengthy legal discourse. Meetings are held, investigations made, ordinances drafted, opened for public comment, passed and finally posted. All of this legal discourse becomes binding law when and where the signs are posted, when and where the signs become discourses in place. Put more simply, signs are designed by sign makers, they are made in the shops and workplaces of sign makers, and they are taken to the relevant sites, where, finally, they become 'signs in place'.

This is equally true of advertising messages because they are shaped and developed by copywriters in their offices and ultimately placed before potential consumers through different kinds of media, so that their placement becomes accountable in the material world. The notice board saying *'Nude Bathing Prohibited'* has the same words, the same sentences and cites the same ordinances while it is riding in the back of the truck of the worker taking it to the beach, where it is to be posted. During this time, the sign may have abstract linguistic meaning, but it does not have any binding 'in place' meaning until it is actually posted firmly in its place on the beach.

Language indexes the world in many ways. The most frequently noted indexicals are personal pronouns ('I', 'we', 'you'), demonstratives ('this', 'that'), deictics ('here', 'there', 'now') and tenses. Our understanding of both spoken utterances and written texts must be anchored in the material world. To understand a sentence such as *"Would you take this over there?"*, we need a provisional location for 'me' (the speaker—a meaning for 'here'), for 'you' (my addressee), for the object ('this'), and for the intended goal ('there'). Our interpretation of demonstratives depends on whether or not we can establish what in the real world is being indexed. Likewise, personal pronouns must look to the context for their interpretation. Who is saying 'I'? Where is the gaze directed when the speaker says 'you'? Deictic adverbs take their meaning from some common and presupposed reference point, which is the only basis for interpretation. When the speaker says, *"We won't have time to do that now"*, does he mean within the next sentence or two, within this social event, or within this calendar year? A mother says to her child, *"We'll do*

that sometime", and the child retorts, *"I know what 'sometime'
means—it means never. I want to do it now."*[2]

In a more consistent way, some words in language cannot be
interpreted at all unless the physical context, especially the
physical context of the speaker, is known. Take the sentence: *"I've
been working hard since I came here."* It might mean 'since I came
home from the office today'. It might mean 'since I came back
from my holiday this past summer'. Or, it might even mean 'since
I came back to India from abroad'. To trace just how wide the
scope of the meaning of 'here' is depends on further
contextualisations.

Some sentences of English are virtually impossible to understand if we do not know who is speaking about whom, where and
when. These sentences contain a large number of deictic expressions, the interpretation of which depends on the immediate
physical context in which they were uttered. Such expressions are
very obvious examples of bits of language, which we can only
understand in terms of the speaker's intended, meaning. If
someone says, *"I love doing that"*, does he mean 'playing tennis',
'flirting with girls', 'partying with friends', 'teaching young
students', or something else entirely? The word, 'that', is a deictic
expression (a means of pointing with language), which can only be
interpreted in terms of the locations that the speaker intends to
indicate.

Coca-Cola came up with an impressive ad line: *'Life Ho To
Aisi'*. This discourse is an instance of code switching. It consists of
words from two languages: It begins with the English noun, 'life',
and ends with the Hindi demonstrative, 'aisi'. All these words
help the writer to convey the thematic meaning of the discourse.
The code-switched words also help the writer to organise the
message in terms of focus and emphasis. Nowadays, code
switching is a popular device in the advertising business. It is
employed for various reasons: to attract the reader's attention, to
make its message more impressive and, thereby, stimulate the
reader to buy the product. In this discourse, the Hindi

demonstrative, 'aisi' ('this'), does need to be interpreted in connection with its existence in the real world.

Personal pronouns index the world of people and social relationships through which we move, much like the demonstratives index the physical spaces in which we live. It is essential in social situations to monitor constantly who is within the current social gathering and who is outside it. When we are having a conversation at dinner in a restaurant, there is a clear difference in the currently ratified conversational roles between the diners at the table and the waiter who comes to take an order or to deliver the ordered dishes. If one of the diners says, *"Would you please give me another fork?"*, everyone at the table knows that it is the waiter who is being addressed. Similarly, the statement, *"Please give me another chance"*, is likely to be understood as a more intimate statement for a dinner partner to hear and respond to, by the waiter, even if he should be within hearing range.[3]

We can see the message of discourse in a series of ads called India Shining, produced by the Government of India. In these ads, the government highlighted its achievements and all that it has done for its citizens in the five years of its rule. The body text of the ad is quite comprehensive and attempts to describe the opportunities and benefits the government has offered the citizens. One of the ads runs thus:

Times are exciting

Villages are progressing

Eyes are twinkling

You've never had

A better time to shine brighter.

The deictic anchorage of the personal pronoun in another line, *"Build your dreams, spread the enthusiasm and make India stronger and shine even better"*, serves to establish a personal rapport with the readers. The above text says in strong words that this is the best time for you to realise your dreams and aspirations. The words, *"You've never had a better time to shine brighter"*, presuppose that the earlier period was not as inspiring and conducive to growth or to 'shine brighter', The bottom line of the India Shining ad is Indian people and their will to grow and how this is best supported by the current government. The ad has a visual featuring an old man from rural India, with bright eyes and a broad smile on his face. The visual of the ad is well-balanced in terms of the overtones of self-respect and honour.

An ad for Philips, a multinational company that produces electronic goods, uses the personal pronoun in its tagline: *'Let's Make Things Better'*. This utterance, in the form of a request, makes a personal bond with the consumers ('Let's'). The strategy is to make an intimate proposition so that the consumers can buy into the product.

In an advertisement for Moods condoms, the discourse is very bold and sensual in its appeal. The ad concerns itself with the addressor's own subjective feelings. It is an expository communication act, which creates ripples in every stage of the discourse.

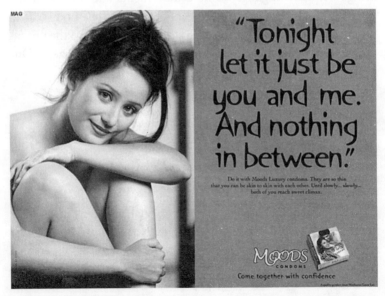

The message of the discourse is quite direct and persuasive as is reflected in the text:

> *Tonight*
>
> *let it just be*
>
> *you & me.*
>
> *And nothing*
>
> *in between.*
>
> *Do it with Moods Luxury condoms. They are so thin that you can be skin to skin with each other. Until slowly ... slowly ... both of you reach sweet climax.*
>
> *Moods*
>
> *Condom*
>
> *Come together with confidence.*

The setting of the discourse in the ad is quite private and personal and the location seems to be the bedroom. The discourse is confined mainly to two passionate lovers. Again the personal pronouns ('you' and 'me') must be analysed in the context of the social relationships in which they perform their actions. These personal pronouns index our social relationship in the material world. Further, advertising messages often use words and groups that can be interpreted both figuratively and literally. The word, 'nothing', is being used at the semantic level in the ad. It says, 'and nothing in between', though there is something, a Moods condom. The idea implied is that a Moods condom is so thin and light that sex using it is like having unprotected sex.

Geoffrey Leech says: "In informative or reasoned discourse, ambiguity is usually considered a fault to be eliminated. In poetry, on the contrary, it is usually treated as a means of enriching the communicative responses of the language, by superimposition or juxtaposition of alternative interpretations."[4] The visual of the Moods ad is attractive and suggests how a young beautiful modern woman exhibits her sexual attitudes plainly and frankly.

When a speaker uses demonstratives and deictic adverbs in normal circumstances, he is working on the assumption that the hearer knows which location or direction is intended. In a more general way, speakers continually design their linguistic messages on the basis of assumptions about what their hearers already know. These assumptions may be mistaken, of course, but they underlie much of what we say in the everyday use of language. What a speaker assumes is true or is known by the hearer can be described as a presupposition.

An ad for the Kawasaki Bajaj Eliminator poses a question to the readers: *"Do you remember who was the second man on the moon?"* This statement is an example of an indirect speech act, but it presupposes that before the 'second man' went on the moon, there was someone else who was the first there. The discourse has a connotative meaning here. The question it poses does not require an answer. Rather, it wants to prove that however great a milestone may be, if it is achieved second, it is too insignificant to remember.

The ad then proceeds to answer the question with great elegance:

There can be only one original.
Kawasaki Bajaj
Eliminator.

The implication is that all other motorbike models may be impressive, but they are merely clones of the original one, the Kawasaki Bajaj Eliminator.

John J. Gumperz remarks, "A basic assumption is that this channelling of interpretation is effected by conversational implicatures, based on conventionalised co-occurrence expectations between content and surface style. That is, constellations of surface features of the message form are the means by which the speakers signal and listeners interpret what the activity is, how semantic content is to be understood and how each sentence relates to what precedes or follows. These features are referred to as contextualisation cues."[5]

In other words, a contextualisation cue is any feature of linguistic form that contributes to the signalling of contextual presuppositions, Although contextualisation cues carry information, meanings are conveyed as part of the interactive process. Unlike words that can be discussed out of context, the meanings of contextualisation cues are implicit. We can take two examples from Gumperz that explain the unverbalised perceptions and presuppositions that underlie interpretation.

Example 1

A husband is sitting in his living room and addressing his wife. The husband belongs to a middle-class American background, the wife is British. They have been married and living in the US for a number of years:

Husband:	Do you know where today's paper is?
Wife:	I'll get it for you.
Husband:	That's OK. Just tell me where it is. I'll get it.
Wife:	No, I'll get it.

The husband is using a question, which, literally interpreted, enquires about the location of the paper. The wife does not reply directly, but offers to get the paper. Her 'I'll' is accented and could be interpreted as "I'll, if you don't". The husband counter-suggests that he was asking for information, not making a request. He also stresses, 'I'll'. The wife then reiterates her statement to emphasise that she intends to get the newspaper. The 'I'll' is now highly stressed to suggest increasing annoyance.

Example 2

A mother is talking to her eleven year old son who is about to go out in the rain:

Mother: Where are your boots?
Son: In the closet.
Mother: I want you to put them on right now.

The mother asks a question, which, literally interpreted, concerns the location of her son's boots. When he responds with a statement about their location, the mother retorts with a direct request. Her stress on 'right now' suggests that she is annoyed at her son for not responding to her initial question as a request in the first place. When a speaker does not know something and asks the hearer to inform him, he will typically produce a direct speech act of the following type: "Can you drive a car?" Now, we can compare this utterance with: "Will you pass the salt?" It is not a question about an ability to do something. In fact, it is not a question at all. We would treat it as a request and perform the action as requested. This is described as an indirect speech act. Perhaps, the crucial distinction in the use of these two types of speech acts is based on the fact that indirect commands or requests are simply considered gentler or more polite in our society than direct commands.

Gumperz writes, "Psychologists, sociolinguists and linguists concerned with understanding discourses all agree that interpretation of longer stretches of text involves simultaneous processing of information at several levels of generality. That is, in determining what is meant at any one point in a conversation, we rely on schemata or interpretive frames based on our experience with similar situations as well as on grammatical and lexical knowledge. Such frames enable us to distinguish among permissible interpretive options. Among other things, they also help in identifying overall themes, in deciding what weight to assign to a particular message segment, and in distinguishing key points from subsidiary or qualifying information."[6] In conversation, information about interpretive schemata is conveyed both through sentence content and through such matters of form as choice of pronunciation, dialect or speech style. We can come across a group of conversationalists and, without understanding actual words, get a fairly accurate idea of what they are saying.

BILT, an established paper brand, advertises its product (paper) without making any utterances in the advertisement. The

Passion. Excitement. Dream.

Commitment. Belief. Focus.

Innovate. Integrity. Success.

Achievement. Valour. Progress.

Confidence. Expand. Honour.

Truth. Vivacious. Leadership.

Spirit. Dare. Exuberant.

Knowledge. Discover...

BILT Royal C2S coated paper gloss 170 gsm.

two-page ad is unique in its presentation. The ad becomes special because not a single sentence is communicated in favour of buying BILT paper. A collection of words has been chosen impressively to establish the identity of the brand and reflect the high quality of the paper. The words speak a lot about the attitude the brand carries within it.

All these words have a positive semantic value. But, the last word, 'Discover ...', takes the reader to the next page where we find the following lines:

A new vision.

A new outlook.

And a new logo reflecting its essence.

bilt

... ideas in paper.

The first time that we notice that this is an ad for BILT paper is when we hit the second page. This is also the first time the name of the brand or the product is used in the discourse. The fact that information of this type can turn up in people's attempts to remember the text is further evidence of the existence of schemata.

It is also a good indication of the fact that our understanding of what we read does not come directly from the words and sentences on a page, but from the interpretation we create in our minds of what we read.

Now look at an ad issued in the public interest by the Centre for Plastics in Environment. There are huge protests against the use of plastics in our daily lives. The Centre for Plastics comes out verbally in favour of the use of plastics, pointing out that it is indispensable because of its multiple roles. It makes people aware of how to use plastics responsibly. The use of plastics carries a negative connotation in society today and a discourse of this nature would really make people change their views about its use. This particular ad has the following constituents:

- The situation
- The problem
- The solution
- The evaluation of the solution

The situation in the discourse is: Attack plastics. Do not use plastics. This situation or problem is to be handled with effective action in the discourse: People should be made aware of the importance of plastic in everyday life. This action is further supported by a suitable solution: Plastics are easily recyclable. Finally, there's a generalisation along with this solution in the discourse: A material that adds so many benefits to our life needs a concerned and responsible attitude from everyone. The advertisement ends with the emphatic message:

You can't live without plastics,
Live with plastics. Responsibly.

The ad holds tremendous visual appeal. It presents the top part of a scene in an operation theatre, where everything is seen to be made out of plastic, including heart valves, saline bottles, blood pouches, equipment, machines and even the doctors' aprons and headgear. Perhaps, that is why plastics are called lifesavers.

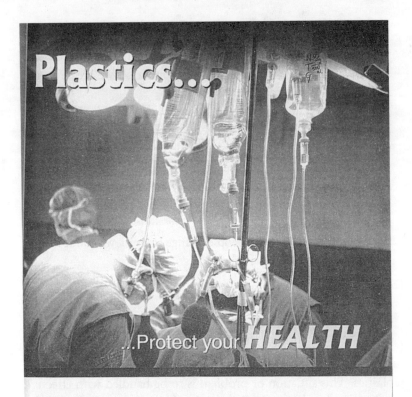

Plastics...

...Protect your *HEALTH*

A life-saver under attack.

Allegations are being made today that plastics are harmful to your health and safety. In actual fact, plastics help protect your health. Plastic syringes, heart valves, catheters and tubes are the modern products doctors depend on. In fact, plastics are the materials that safely carry the blood that may one day save your life. When used in packaging, plastics protect against germs, prevent dangerous cross-contamination and bacterial spread and are critical for a host of healthcare products. Far from being the culprits, plastics are the great protectors - invaluable today for a range of applications in our daily lives.

Today's technology makes plastics easily recyclable. Plastics don't pollute - we do. A material that adds so many benefits to our life needs a concerned and responsible attitude from everyone.

ICPE
Recycle Recover Reuse

You can't live without plastics.
Live with plastics. Responsibly.

An underlying assumption in most conversations seems to be that the participants are, in fact, cooperating with each other. Paul Grice points out that conversation is a cooperative activity in which the participants, in order to infer what is intended, must reconcile what they hear with what they understand to be the immediate purpose of the activity. He formulates the cooperative principle: "Make your contribution such as is required at the stage at which it occurs by the accepted purpose or direction of the talk exchange in which you are engaged." He lists four subcategories and related maxims in terms of which the cooperative principle is articulated in particular instances: quantity—make your contribution as informative as necessary; quality—be truthful; relation—be relevant with reference to what is being talked about; and manner—avoid obscurity and ambiguity and obey proper form. An out of circulation ad for Parle-G glucose biscuits illustrates the cooperative principle in discourse:

> *Housewife: Shakkar laaye?(Have you got the sugar?)*
> *Servant: Nahin, ji. (No, ji.)*
> *Housewife: Chai patti?(Tea leaves?)*
> *Servant: Nahin, ji. (No, ji.)*
> *Housewife: Phir kya laaye?(Then what did you get?)*
> *Servant: Parle-G.*

The discourse is very brief, clear and orderly. It fulfils all the requirements of the cooperative principle. At the end of the discourse, the housewife is a little irritated, but soon becomes all right when the servant says, "Parle-G."

We shall examine how objects are constituted as visual wholes, whether two-dimensional pictures or sculpted figures, in the semiotics of visual space. The term, 'visual semiotics', refers to the work of Gunther Kress and Theo Van Leeuwen, particularly as found in their book, *Reading Images: The Grammar of Visual Design.* They analyse the compositional interpretations of experience and different forms of social interaction. This 'grammar of visual design' is intended as a step toward training in 'visual literacy', which they see as quickly becoming a matter of survival in contemporary life, at the workplace in particular. Though global to the extent of being spread all over the globe, their visual semiotic is not universal, but culturally specific, with a history of some five centuries in Western culture. With their examples of paintings, photographs, diagrams and, thus, two-dimensional representations, as well as sculptures, they hope to stimulate the study of visual communication in non-Western societies, anticipating that elements such as central or margin, top or bottom will convey meaning and values differently where writing proceeds from right to left or top to bottom.

We also notice some such activities when visual images play an important role in their interpretation. When Bajaj Auto Ltd launched the Pulsar motorbike, it was advertised as a tough bike with masculine features. The ad for the Pulsar had an interesting tagline, *'Definitely Male'*, but the actual macho quality of the motorbike was observed in its TV commercial, reflected in a visual semiotic. When two beautiful young nurses walk past the static motorbike, its handlebars and headlights turn towards them automatically, just like a man would turn his head towards the girls to get a better look.

An ad for Tata Yellow Pages features the body language and facial expressions of the father of a newborn baby. The man, who has just had a first look at the baby, is shocked because the baby does not resemble either him or his wife. The couple is extremely fair, charming and very Indian by appearance but the child, on the other hand, closely resembles an American African. The man is dismayed. What should he do? Immediately, there flashes on the TV screen the line: *'Do You Need a Divorce Lawyer?'*

The Scollons signify the concept of emplacement as the most fundamental issue of geosemiotics. The geosemiotic meaning of the sign defends where on the earth it is placed or located. A sign showing a lighted cigarette within a slashed red circle is universally taken to mean *'No Smoking'*, but it is only by reference of the physical location of the sign that we know where not to smoke. The reading is based on where in space the sign is found. In some cases, both time and place are important for correct interpretation. A sign may be placed on a highway which indicates that a business establishment is ten minutes ahead. This implies not only the directionality of travel, but the speed. One cannot walk there in ten minutes.

Coca-Cola uses a line in its signboard ad: *'Panch Matlab Chota Coke'*. When we read the signboard, we do not feel convinced that 'panch' (five) has the same unified application all over the world. *'Panch Matlab Chota Coke'* is not a dictionary meaning or something that is taught to children in a school. It is an advertising master inventing new meanings and giving different expressions to such phrases through the ad. Here, the statement is not meant for universal acceptance, rather its meaning can be traced in relation to its physical context. It encompasses the concept of emplacement, where the sign or text can be understood in the context of its placement in the physical world. 'Panch' does not have the same meaning anytime, anywhere. The line, *'Panch Matlab Chota Coke'*, is relevant only at the retail counter where a Coke is sold.

The Scollons categorise three systems of emplacement: 'decontextualised', 'transgressive' and 'situated'. Decontextualised semiotics includes all the forms of signs, pictures and texts that may appear in multiple contexts, but always in the same form. The Nike 'swoosh', the characteristic Coca-cola typeface and the golden arches of McDonald's are all decontextualised signs that may appear in the same form on posters, packages of the products, or on the hoardings of stores in which these products are sold. Brand names and logos, which produce universal and decontextualised recognition of their products, are the best examples of decontextualised semiotics.

Transgressive semiotics includes any sign that is in the wrong place or violates the convention on emplacement in some way or the other. We know that a Jockey inner wear sticker stuck on a bathroom door does not denote the size of the bathroom door because we know it as a meaning that is out of place. A transgressive sign is a sign which is in place, but which is unauthorised in some way or the other, such as graffiti, trash or discarded items.

Situated semiotics is any aspect of the meaning that is predicted on the placement of the sign in the material world. Here, a sign is shaped by and shapes the material world in which it is placed. Thus, an exit sign derives its meaning from the exit and the exit is found because of the sign.

Notes

1. McCarthy, Michael, 2001. 'Discourse', in Ronald Carter and David Nunan (eds), *Cambridge Guide to Teaching English to Speakers of Other Languages*. Cambridge: Cambridge University Press, p. 48.

2. Scollon, Ron, and Suzie Scollon, 2003. *Discourse in Place: Language in the Material World*. London: Routledge, Taylor & Francis Group, pp. 31–32.

3. Ibid., p. 36.

4. Leech, Geoffrey N., 1966. *English in Advertising*. London: Longman Green & Co. Ltd., p. 184

5. Gumperz, J. John, 1982. *Discourse Strategies*. Cambridge: Cambridge University Press, p. 131.

6. Ibid., pp. 21–22.

Six

The Semiotics of Visual Communication in Print Advertisements

Words, like nature, half reveal
And half conceal the soul within.

— Alfred, Lord Tennyson

Advertisements are everywhere. On the bus, in the city, in the streets, in the movies, in our mail, in our SMSes, these powerful images follow us wherever we go. Billions of dollars are spent on advertising every year. Out of these billions are born the messages that tell us where to invest, what to wear, what to eat, how to get slim, how to gain weight and so much more. They claim to offer solutions to anything that we find difficult in our lives. More than this, they shape our everyday plans and decisions. A baby crying for its feed, a young executive flaunting a new car, a dusky girl applying a fairness cream and a housewife looking longingly at a new sari are all advertisements because they all indicate desirability. They want to communicate, to persuade, to influence and to lead to some action. Thus, advertising has become a strong force in our economic and social lives.

Being a study of human behaviour and responses, advertising is subject to unpredictability and very few clear answers. Its answers are at best probabilistic and never ever universal truths. As advertising is a lot about strong images and perceptions, the intensity of the imagery is quite understandable. Apart from the intense imagery, advertising also generates a number of heated debates and 'opinions' among people because having opinions and expressing them is part and parcel of being human. The

BECAUSE PAIN IS BIGGER AND YOU ARE SMALLER

subjectivity of such opinions will also continue. After all, advertising is seen and felt by most of us in our 'personal' domains, what we can identify with (what we like) and what we cannot (what we don't like).[1] We live in a symbol-rich environment, where we must construct meaning from a plethora of images. In an ad for Panadol, a paracetamol based analgesic which provides fast, effective, temporary relief from pain and discomfort, a baby is shown crying in pain and looking tired and helpless. The simple baseline, *'Because Pain is Bigger and You are Smaller'*, connects the painful expression of the baby with the brand value. It communicates how Panadol works to provide relief as no one can see the tears on the baby's face. The visual and the message are together a perfect piece of creativity, which captivates the heart and soul of the reader. A crucial distinction in the semiotic analysis of signs is between the signifier and the signified. The signifier, as, for instance, a brand name like Panadol, has no meaning in its own right, but must acquire meaning through associations with some other pre-existing meaning (the instant relief or suffering of a child, in this case) until it comes to signify some concept or idea.

This chapter seeks to look at how visual messages are formed and given meaning through a semiotic analysis of advertisements. The practitioners of the semiotic school believe that the meanings of pictures are not in the pictures, but in what we bring to them. Since visual interpretation is based upon perception through cognition and language and is affected by social, cultural and personal frames, we strongly believe that semiotics will help us explain the complexity of visual communication while processing visual information and producing meaning from the advertisements. This concept of visual semiotics is the major driving force in this chapter. The primary goal is to establish the underlying conventions and identify the significant differences and oppositions in an attempt to model the system of categories, relations (syntagmatic and paradigmatic), connotations, distinctions and rules of combination employed.

The meanings of the images that we see in most ads are hard to decipher. To a humble consumer, reality is always elusive. If we study the ads, we may be able to 'look into' them to unfold social and cultural realities. We learn from semiotics that we live in a world of signs, and we have no way of understanding anything except through signs and the codes into which they are organised. Through the study of semiotics, we become aware that these signs and codes are normally transparent and disguise our task in 'reading' them.[2] It is important to talk here of the basic theory of semiotics, which inspired me

to decipher the visual images of a few advertisements. The writings of Ferdinand De Saussure and Charles S. Pierce are the fundamental works for the semiotic study of advertising images and help us in reading the hidden meanings and underlying current of advertising signs. A sign can be a word, a sound or a visual image. It is an object which stands for another to some minds. Saussure divides a sign into two components: the signifier (the sound, image or word) and the signified, which is the concept the signifier represents, or the meaning.

Pierce, who is called the founder of American semiotics, disagrees with Saussure on the arbitrariness condition. To Pierce, signs are of three types: icons, indexes and symbols. There are just three ways a sign, such as a word, a sentence, a picture, a graph or a gesture, can have meaning in semiotic theory. It can be a picture of a thing in the world. This is called an icon. The little picture of a happy face made by email and mobile phone users, using a colon and right parentheses – :) – is an icon. It shows a schematic picture of a smiling face.

A sign can also be a completely arbitrary representation of a thing in the world. This would be called a symbol. A green traffic light means we can continue driving. There is nothing inherent in the colour green that 'means' move ahead or keep going. It is an arbitrary association.

Finally, a sign means something because of where and when it is located in the world. In this case, it is called an index. An index is a sign. An arrow pointing in one direction down a street is an index which shows the exact direction in which traffic should go.[3]

Advertising as a system consists of distinct signs, and what an advertiser means depends on how the signs he uses are organised. Semiotics seeks to discover how the meaning of an advertisement

does not simply float on the surface waiting to be understood by consumers.

Let us take up the first Marlboro advertisement for semiotic analysis. The ad predominantly features a macho male model, dressed in cowboy (a macho occupation) gear. Adjacent to him is an iconic image of Marlboro cigarettes, which are thus projected as the secret of the heroic deeds deemed to have been performed by the male model. Amongst these images, we find a signified linguistic concept in the form of a verbal message: *'Come to Where*

the Flavour Is'. It is difficult to ignore this powerful iconic image of the quintessential American cowboy, who stands for adventure, freedom and fearlessness. The print ad is designed with a purpose: to create an image of a Marlboro Man—an icon that is an antithesis of an ordinary man. A cowboy signifies an environment that is challenging, natural and relatively stress-free. He is his own man in a world he owns. Two images are very prominent in the ad: First, that the subject—the image of the macho man—provides a youthful element of glamour and adventure, which serves both the product and the text in which it is being advertised, and second, that the image of the Marlboro countryside is a physical acknowledgement of the product name. However, these images alone certainly do not convey this central signified concept, for this is only guaranteed by the inclusion of the tagline, *'Come to Where the Flavour Is'*. Thus, a strong relationship is allowed to emerge between the 'signifiers' (the photographic image of the Marlboro Man and his physical environment) and the 'signified' (the linguistically expressed *'Come to Where the Flavour Is'*). The linguistic sign is very meaningful here in leading the target audience to the desired results.

The word, 'flavour', has its own layers of meaning. While there is no logical connection between the cowboy and the smoking experience, the composition of the ad, the colour scheme, the aura of the iconic cowboy and the verbal message depict a realistic world in which the pleasant experience of smoking is linked to Marlboro cigarettes. The advertisers work at every stage to create maximum impact for the advertised product. The striking element I found in the

Marlboro cigarettes pack was the two letters 'l' and 'b' standing taller than the rest in the brand name, and their serifs resembling smoke.

Fred Inglis writes that cigarette marketing, packaging and advertising offer a central topic for any study of advertising. Not only are cigarettes utterly expendable and very dangerous, they are also dirty, smelly and unsightly. Consequently, a great deal of cigarette advertising goes in for fresh, wholesome scenery. The associations of this picture (setting aside the subconscious and economic ones) are clean and uncontaminated. Whatever the reality of offshore sewage, the sea is poetically bracing and salty.[4]

Let us move on to the next set of print ads. Shown here is a print ad for Aesthetis Clinic. I appreciate the element of creativity shown by the advertiser in communicating a simple business message artistically in this ad. I feel that the design of the entire ad is, possibly, the most innovative way to obtain the consumers' attention and lead them to purchase the product in question. The visual of the Aesthetis Clinic ad is extremely eye-catching and distinct; the use of colours, text and photography are all key

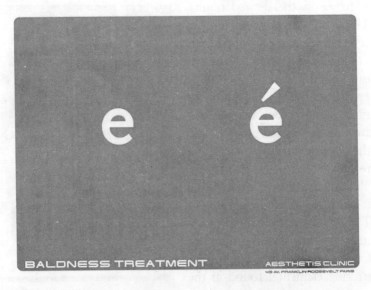

factors in making it persuasive and in awakening the desired emotions, feelings and values in consumers. We have a very different set of symbols in the visual. The first sign, 'e', is a signifier and it symbolises the problem of baldness faced by many people. The sign is unique and in no way apparently resembles the concept of baldness, but the moment we relate this sign to the next sign beside it, an 'e' with an acute accent mark, we understand that the advertiser is smartly working on the emotional weakness of the target audience and elegantly trying to provide a solution in the form of a hairy head.

All signs, whether they are icons or symbols, are indexes. That is because, in order to exist, all signs must be located in the material world. Both signs do not have any meaning in isolation, unless we see them in the context of a linguistic message. The simple and straight verbal sign is an index that shows the existence and relevance of the two signs centrally posed in the visual. The advertiser uses just two symbols and does not want to distract the audience from the overall impact of the advertising message. The ad is set in a green background and the two symbols and textual signs are shown in white. The green colour symbolises productivity, prosperity and happiness—the ultimate solution offered by the advertisers in the form of new hair growth on the scalp, while the authenticity of the business purpose is further endorsed by the white colour, which denotes purity, truthfulness and an acknowledgement of the advertising claims made by the marketer.

Generally, colour is used to disguise a fact or to identify the key features of a product. Marketers feel that colour sells and the right colour sells better. Colour is the first thing that attracts people emotionally to a product or a space. It speaks to the subconscious, evokes feelings and meanings and moods, and has an incredible ability to influence buying behaviour. This is a huge subject and a matter of much debate for marketers.[5]

The next ad is one for Coca-Cola. It shows a picture of a hair salon, where two people are being given hair-cuts. Interestingly, the only visible link that we develop between the signifier (the

bottle of Coca-Cola filled with water) and the signified (the cooling, soothing experience of having your hair cut) is the person holding the bottle of Coca-Cola filled with water. We can see the brand name on the bottle which the barber is using to spray water on the head of his client. Although this print ad appears to be simple, its connotative meanings allow our interpretation of it to be a pragmatic one, in that its signifiers have particular relevance with regard to the context of the ad. If we observe closely, we notice through the windows that it is summer and no one is out on the street; consequently, the linguistic sign, 'Thanda Matlab Coca-Cola', is an index that is rightly connected to the outside environment. Here, the brand, Coca-Cola, is associated with the cooling impact of the drink and reinforces the verbal message that any activity in the scorching heat with Coca-Cola will provide comfort and satisfaction. Although the bottle is empty, the company is highlighting the cooling experience ensured to a consumer, no matter what he does with a Coca-Cola. The advertiser wishes to convey the idea of 'Thanda Matlab Coca-Cola' and uses the sign indexically in a social context. As with all indexical signs, there is a bond between the signifier (the bottle) and the signified (the refreshing experience of having a haircut in the summer). The colour of the product name, Coca-Cola, is red and it provides a strong connection between the product and its commercial message.

The next ad we shall look at is for Hutch mobile phone services. The ad is strikingly visual and, with its visual representation, it elucidates the basic message that underlines SMS services. The visual consists of different alphabets and their visual forms. The visual signifies that every alphabet stands for a new abbreviated form of spelling that can be used in SMS messages. For example the letter 'A' stands for apple, but in the ad, the emphasis is on learning the short and simple spellings for existing standard words. That is why the world 'apple' is rewritten as *'apl'* and 'butterfly' as *'bttrfly'*, and so on. With the emphasis on the new

experience of SMS language, the print ad encourages the audience to take the message the way it is presented and finally associates the visual with the textual part of the message: *'SMS. The New Language'*. What it means here is that the advertiser is using language cleverly in a visual image so that he can persuade the audience to buy and accept the new advertising concept, which is the ad's sole aim.

The next print ad that I am taking up for semiotic analysis promotes social consciousness for our environment by asking

Save Trees. Trees Save.

people to save trees. The ad comes with a strong visual and a sincere message to keep trees—and our environment—intact. The impact is very high because we can see the scene of a natural calamity in the form of a flood, where the entire area is submerged in water and the lone man in the picture is perched in a tree. The flood is a prominent signifier of the careless attitude of human beings towards nature. It is interesting to note that the man on the tree, who represents the entire human civilisation, seems to be desperate and helpless now, in the aftermath of his reckless misuse of natural resources. There is also a strong connection between the visual and the textual message. On the extreme top right, the advertiser says: 'Save Trees. Trees Save'. The message is clear: If we care for nature, nature will care for us. The tall image of the tree on which the man seeks shelter is indexical to the real world in which nature always cares, protects and guides human beings. The grim photographical representation of the flooded area in black and white are additional signifiers of how society is moving forward callously, without any thought for nature. The ad symbolically demonstrates that man and nature are closely inter-dependent.

Designers of print ads usually use photographs along with minimal linguistic material. The print ad we will take up now is one for *Veja* magazine, which beautifully employs a 'one word image' to create the maximum persuasive effect for the product advertised. When we see and study the ad, we find a single word, '*bomb*', in black letters against a yellow background. The style in which the word, 'bomb', is spelt and designed in the ad gives a visual impression of a real bomb. The symbol (bomb) stands in isolation on the surface level, but what the advertiser expects the audience to find hidden in the '*bomb*' image is the word, '*bluff*', which is enveloped in the first word. Once the readers get through these two signifiers, the ad will lead them to the product and its philosophy, which are signified by these two words. The two signs signify that *Veja* offers its readers both sides of a story and provides in-depth analysis of issues. The ad does not reflect that the linguistic sign ('bomb') is intentionally and systematically designed in such a way that it may also project the other sign ('bluff') within it. This is a common trend in advertising media in

order to achieve an even greater and more pervasive effect on the consumer.

One must view the manipulation of linguistic entities as a type of 'foregrounding'. Foregrounding is a linguistic process in which some elements, such as words, phrases, sentences, stresses, intonations and the like, are given prominence or made more meaningfully significant by the communicator or language user, in this case the creator(s) of the print ad for *Veja*.[6] When we index our image ('bomb') to the real situation (*Veja*), we get to know that the magazine's cover story talks about North Korea's intention to test atomic bombs—that's the reason that the rest of the world and the media sense a 'bomb'; they do not consider it a 'bluff'. The concern of the majority is voiced in the form of 'bomb' in a bold black font.

The cosmetics sector has often been accused of using advertising to impose impossible standards of beauty and thereby contributing to the problem of self-esteem among women and girls. Fair & Lovely launched its campaign for a 'fair complexion' to appeal to women whose appearance did not match traditional standards of beauty. However, the concept of 'magic skin' is no

longer restricted to the female domain, for even men are being targeted now. This ad for the Nivea for Men skincare range shows a sports stadium, where a group of footballers are defending a shot from the opposition. The players are standing with their hands raised to cover their faces, rather than their groins, as one would expect. The players standing in that particular position are the major signifiers of the problem posed in the print ad—the harmful effect of the sun on the players' skin. The players do not want to take a chance. The visual image shows not a single stain or spot on the clothes of the players, which denotes their predilection for cleanliness and skin care. In this ad, the signifier is the bunch of players covering their faces and the signified object is the Nivea for Men skincare range, which stands tall in white, offering the right solution for sportsmen with sensitive skin. There is one sign in the ad, which is invisible, but the presence of which is felt even in its absence—there is no opponent striker ready to take a shot. But the audience hits upon the underlying meaning by understanding the other visible signs.

The ultimate objective of advertising efforts is to gain more consumers to ensure growth and long-term profits. The magic mirror of advertising works like any ordinary mirror in that it lets consumers see their own image in the mirror (of advertising). The 'magic' happens only when, unlike in an ordinary mirror, they see themselves not as what they are, but as what they want to be. By playing up wants and aspirations, advertising makes the brand desirable.[7]

While maintaining their supremacy in international markets, successful global players localise their advertising messages to become unique, saleable and relevant to the local conditions. This print ad for McDonald's 100 per cent Vegetarian Festival shaped its message according to local needs to win over Indian consumers. The ad shows a South Indian pundit (priest) with religious marks on his forehead, except that the marks on his forehead form the golden arches of McDonald's. The sign is a strong indicator of McDonald's commitment to the glocalisation of its advertising

message. The sign on the priest's forehead signifies the linguistic sign (The 100% Vegetarian Festival) shown on the top right of the print ad. The brand, McDonald's, shows its solidarity with the people of the nation by keeping its outlets completely vegetarian during festive seasons.

The last print ad that I'm taking up for semiotic analysis is another Panadol ad. The visual of the ad is attractive and features a well-known father-son pair, former US presidents George H.W. Bush and George W. Bush. They are shown in a cheerful mood, enjoying golf. Their very personas show power, sophistication and freedom in real life. What is interesting here is the linguistic sign ('*One is Enough*') denoted by the two men. The pun is intended to achieve a dramatic effect and gain more consumers' attention. The message ('*One is Enough*') has two layers of meaning—what it says explicitly on the surface and what it contains implicitly. It is left to the audience to decide what one is enough for—to get rid of pain or to generate pain. In other words, whether one Panadol is enough to relieve pain or one Bush is enough to give pain to the world, is the crux of the advertising message. The so-called ambiguous sentences testify to the existence of deep structures. How does one know that a sentence has more

than one sense? The surface arrangement is just the same, the signs received are identical, and yet the meaning could be very different. It is Noam Chomsky's thesis that while the surface structure is identical in all interpretations, the deep structure is not. The diverse meanings of ambiguous sentences are realised when proper and different deep structures are evoked.[8]

Advertising fascinates people. It flirts momentarily with their lives, seduces them and leaves them with wonderful images and dreams. In order to be fulfilled, these dreams make people work harder, earn more and spend more. Advertising is an integral part of our social and economic systems. In our complex society, advertising has evolved into a vital communication system for both consumers and businesses. The interpretation of visual images is very subjective and thus cannot be conclusive as images are open to different renditions. In order to understand visual communication, it is expected that the audience or consumer have sound critical thinking ability. Our senses, instincts, cultural settings and values greatly affect the process of visual interpretation. Even our personal life, background, moods and needs contribute significantly to the interpretation process. I find the semiotic analysis of print ads interesting and challenging because no single image has a fixed meaning and comprehension depends completely on how the signs function and organise their value within the ad and in the context of its audience and product.

Notes

1. Tiwari, Sanjay, 2003. *The (Un)common Sense of Advertising: Getting the Basics Right.* New Delhi: Response Books, p. 23.

2. Chandler, Daniel, 1994. June 6, 2007. *http://www.aber.ac.uk/media/Documents/S4B/.*

3. Inglis, Fred, 1972. *The Imagery of Power: A Critique of Advertising.* London: Heinemann Educational Books Ltd., p. 92.

4. Scollon, Ron, and Suzie Scollon, 2003. *Discourse in Place: Language in the Material World.* London: Routledge, Taylor & Francis Group.

5. Nair, Anita G., 2007. 'What Does Colour Say about Your Brand?', in *The Times of India,* New Delhi. October 20, p. 20.

6. Harris, Allan C. January 15, 2006. *http://www.csun.edu/ ~ vcspc005/advertis.html.*

7. Tiwari, Sanjay, 2003. *The (Un)common Sense of Advertising: Getting the Basics Right.* New Delhi: Response Books, p. 120.

8. Langholz, Leymore V., 1975. *Hidden Myth: Structure and Symbolism in Advertising.* London: Heinemann.

Seven

Information Technology and Advertising Language

To err is human, but to really foul things up requires a computer.

The Internet is one of most remarkable things human beings have ever made. In terms of its impact on society, it ranks with print, the railways, the telegraph, automobiles, electric power and television. Some would equate it with print and television, the two earlier technologies that most transformed the communications environment in which people live. Yet, it is potentially more powerful than both because it harnesses the intellectual leverage which print gave to mankind without being hobbled by the 'one to many' nature of broadcast television.[1]

With the Internet, information technology has revolutionised the lives of people globally. Within a few years, the Internet has acquired an indispensable status in our society, with email rapidly replacing conventional modes of correspondence. John Naughton talks of the significance of the role of email and says, "The Net was built on electronic mail ... . It's the oil which lubricates the system."[2] The World Wide Web is the first port of call for most types of information inquiry and the first resort for most types of leisure activity. The creator of the web, computer scientist Tim Berner-Lee, defines it as 'the universe of network-accessible information, an embodiment of human knowledge'.[3] The Internet has been an extraordinarily rapid communication revolution.

The Internet is an association of computer networks with common standards, which enable messages to be sent from any central computer (or host) on one network to any host on any other. It is the world's largest computer network, which provides an increasing range of services and enables an unprecedented number of people to be in touch with each other through electronic mail (email) discussion groups and the provision of digital pages on any topic. Functional information such as electronic shopping, business data, advertisements and bulletins can be found alongside creative works, such as poems and scripts. The availability of movies, TV programmes and other kinds of entertainment is also growing steadily. Some commentators have likened the Internet to an amalgam of television, telephone and conventional publishing. The term, 'cyberspace', has been coined to capture the notion of a world of information present or possible in digital form—the information superhighway.[4]

The Internet contains many different situations, says David Crystal, and each situation contains salient linguistic features. In his book, *Language and the Internet*, Crystal looks at five situations: email, synchronous and asynchronous, chat groups, virtual worlds and the World Wide Web. He tries to identify the ways in which they are used. With these five situations, we encounter a new kind of genuine medium. This new medium offers a learning situation of a different kind to people. They must acquire the rules of communicating via email, electronic chatting, constructing an effective Web page, socialising in fantasy roles, and so on, and yet there are no rules in the sense of the universally agreed modes of behaviour established by generations of usage. There is a clear contrast with the world of paper-based communication. We find a sizeable difference in the structure of formal letter writing and email, the Internet equivalent of letter writing. The formal letter writing that we learned in schools is full of do's and don'ts, while email has no such rules.

Today, people feel that the world has become a small village because one can talk to anyone, enter libraries, discuss academic problems, share ideas and search for any kind of information that is not otherwise easily available. They have access to all parts of the world. This has been made possible due to the invention of email, chat groups and the World Wide Web. Recently, a virtual university has been set up without bricks and walls. One need no longer travel to another country to complete one's education. This was not possible earlier, which shows that accessibility has increased.[5]

With the emergence of new communication technologies, there is a widespread debate on the issue of the use of language on the Internet. Some critics believe that technology will rule, standards will be lost and creativity diminished because globalisation imposes sameness. Some people, on the other hand, favour the Internet, saying that it is enabling a dramatic expansion to take place in the range and variety of languages and providing unprecedented opportunities for personal creativity.

The new medium through which we communicate online is called by different names: Netlish, Weblish, Internet language, Cyberspeak, electronic discourse, computer-mediated communication (CMC) and many more. Crystal calls it Netspeak. As a name, Netspeak is succinct and functional enough, as long as we remember that the 'speak' suffix also has a receptive element, including 'listening and reading'.[6] The evolution of Netspeak illustrates a real tension which exists between the nature of the medium and the aims and expectations of its users. The heart of the matter seems to be its relationship to the spoken and written language. Several writers have called Internet language 'written speech' and 'wired style' because, on the Net, as an influential Internet manual says, people *write the way people talk*.

Once we take the different Internet situations into account, the Web is seen to be by far the closest to written language, with chat groups the furthest away, and the other two situations falling in between. The differences are striking, says Crystal, but on the whole, Netspeak is better seen as written language which has been pulled some way in the direction of speech, than as spoken language which has been written down. Although Internet language seems partially similar to both speech and written language, the two are not exactly identical. It is a mix of both forms to some extent as it exhibits certain features of both speech and written language. Netspeak is more than an aggregate of spoken and written features, says Crystal, as it does things that neither of these other media does and, therefore, must be seen as a new species of communication. Writers like Baron use a metaphor for this medium, calling it an 'emerging language centaur—part speech, part writing'.[7] It is more than just a hybrid of speech and writing or the result of contact between two longstanding media.

With all its distinct features, it is emerging as a genuine third medium.

The language we witness on the Internet is distinct and new. When we surf online, we find many neologisms, phrases and expressions which display the uniqueness and novelty of the rapidly growing, computer mediated communication. The language of the Internet is easy, intimate, informal and, to some extent, free from the clutches of grammar. Brevity and innovation are the two buzzwords of this new medium. New jargon and netiquette are increasing gradually. In everyday conversation, terms from the underlying computer technology are given a new application among people who want their conversation to have a cool, cutting edge. Here are some examples from recent overheard conversations:

- *It's my turn to download now (I've heard all your gossip, now listen to mine).*
- *I need more bandwidth to handle that point (I can't take it in all at once).*
- *She's multitasking (She's doing several things at the same time).*
- *Let's go offline for a few minutes (Let's talk in private).*
- *Give me a brain dump on that (Tell me all you know).*
- *I'll ping you later (I'll get in touch to see if you're around).*
- *He's 404 (He's not around).*
- *That's an alt.dot way of looking at things (A cool way).*
- *Are you wired (Are you ready to handle this)?*

Source: David Crystal's Language and the Internet

So, it is a world where many of the participants are highly motivated individualists, intent on exploring the potential of a new medium, with knowledge about its procedures, and holding firm views about the way it should be used. The most informed of this population are young men, who are referred to as 'geeks' in Internet terminology. Geeks are innovative and fun-loving and they like to experiment with developing codes, speaking technolingo and making excessive use of 'slash', 'dot' and 'at' in the medium.

There are several differences between Internet language and face-to-face conversation in all electronic situations. Although, the Internet is electronic, global and interactive, the rhythm of Internet interactions is much slower than that found in a speech situation. Email and asynchronous chat groups on the Internet also disallow some important features of conversation because a response to a stimulus may take anything from seconds to months, the rhythm of the exchange depending on such factors as the recipient's computer (for example, whether it announces the instant arrival of a message), the user's personality and habits (whether messages are replied to at regular times or randomly) and the circumstances of the interlocutors (their computer access). The time delay (usually referred to as lag) is a central factor in many situations, and there is an inherent uncertainty in knowing the length of the gap between the moment of posting a message and the moment of receiving a reaction. Because of this lag, the rhythm of an interaction—even in the fastest Netspeak encounters—in synchronous chat groups and virtual worlds lacks the pace and predictability of telephonic or face-to-face communication.

The most common features of distinction of Netspeak are found chiefly in graphology and the lexicon, levels of language where it is relatively easy to introduce innovation and deviation. Many words relating to computer technology are becoming popular, useful and familiar with users. Internet users use these terms to perform their routine computer work and execute any other commands or computer-related functions. These terms include 'file', 'edit', 'view', 'cut', 'paste', 'insert', 'copy', 'tools', 'windows', 'help', 'search', 'refresh', 'home', 'send', 'open', 'close', 'select' and 'font'. Many terms have been coined just for the Internet, such as 'netizens', 'netters', 'netties', 'netheads', 'cybersurfers', 'newbies', 'surfers' and 'digiterati'. Most of these words are used online every day and have been given a fresh sense in the context of the Internet. Internet language has produced innumerable expressions with an 'e-' prefix, the 'e' standing for electronic. Many of them have found a place even in the *Oxford English Dictionary*. Here is a long list of words starting with 'e', which are quite in vogue today: 'e-zine', 'e-cash', 'e-money', 'e-banking', 'e-lancers', 'e-therapy', 'e-management', 'e-governance', 'e-fair', 'e-mate', 'e-conference', 'e-book', 'e-loan', 'e-pinions', 'e-shop' and 'e-voting'. Journalistic headlines and captions often play with terms in the hope of catching the reader's eye, so it is not surprising to find e-motivated lexical formations in both specialist newspapers and magazines and the general press.[9] Dotcom is now a commonly heard phrase and appears in all kinds of writing and advertising and promotional material. There are also suffixes that are used to show what kind of organisation an electronic address belongs to, such as '.com' (commercial), '.edu' or '.ac' (educational or academic), '.gov' (governmental), '.mil' (military), '.net' (network organisation), and '.org' or '.co' (organisation or company).

Compounding is a common practice among Internet users; this is done by combining two separate words to make a neologism. While creating neologisms, generally, one word comes from Internet-related applications and it is clubbed with any other general word. The word, 'mouse', has a special function in computer applications and it is compounded in many forms ('mouse-click', 'mousepad', 'mouseover') and also as phrasal verbs ('mouse across', 'mouse over'). The word, 'click', is being compounded as 'click and buy', 'one click', 'cost per click', 'double click' and 'click and fly'. Web is another word which attaches itself to others to form many new expressions, such as 'webcam', 'webcast', 'webmail', 'webliography', 'webmaster', 'webnomics' and 'webzine'. Other such words are cyber ('cyberspace', 'cyber culture', 'cyber sin', 'cryber crime', 'cybersex', 'cyber rights') and hyper ('hypertext', 'hyperlink', 'hyper fiction', 'hyperzine'). The symbol, '@', is also enjoying an increasingly prefixal value—'@ party', '@ address', '@ home'—in non-Internet situations. Blends, in which part of one word is joined to part of another, are coming into vogue, too, thanks to Internet language: 'netiquette', 'netizen', 'cyberabad', 'infonent' and 'cybercide'. These word-formation devices are innovative, less time consuming and much in vogue among Internet users.

It becomes extremely difficult for people to live up to the recommendation that they should write as they talk. Internet language varies not only in the domain of the lexicon, but also in prosody and paralanguage-phonological terms expressed through vocal variations in pitch (intonation), loudness (stress), speed, rhythm, pause and tone of voice. To overcome these short-comings, there have been somewhat desperate efforts in the form of an exaggerated use of spelling, punctuation, capitals, spacing and special symbols for added emphasis. Examples include repeated letters ('aaaaahhhh', 'oohhhh', 'hiiiiii', 'soooooory'), repeated punctuations marks ('so what!!!!!!!', 'who he??????', 'see what you done????????') and the following range of emphatic conventions:[10]

All capitals for 'shouting': 'I SAID NO'
Letter spacing for 'loud and clear': 'W H Y N O T W H Y N O T'
Word/phrase emphasis with asterisks: 'the *real* answer'

These features are indeed capable of a certain range of expressions, but the range of meanings they signal is small and restricted to gross notions such as extra emphasis, surprise and puzzlement.

Internet language lacks facial expressions and the gestures and conventions of body posture and distance, which are so critical in experiencing personal opinions and attitudes and in moderating social relationships. This limitation was noticed early in the development of Netspeak and led to the introduction of smileys or emoticons. These are combinations of keyboard characters designed to show an emotional facial expression; they are typed in sequence on a single line and placed after the final punctuation mark of a sentence. Almost all of them are read sideways.

Emoticons have been called 'the paralanguage of the Internet', but they are not the same in that they have to be consciously added to the text. Their absence does not mean that the user lacks the emotion conveyed. In face-to-face communication, someone may grin over several utterances and the effect will be noted. In Netspeak, a 'grin' emoticon might be added to just one utterance, although the speaker may continue to 'feel' the relevant emotion over several utterances. There is also no guarantee that the person who sends a 'grin' is actually grinning. This also applies to the abbreviation, 'LOL'. How many people are actually 'laughing out loud' when they send an 'LOL'?

Examples of Smileys

:-)		Pleasure, humour, etc.
:-(		Sadness, dissatisfaction
;-)		Winking (in any of its meanings)
;-(	:~-(	Crying
%-(	%-)	Confused
:-o	8-o	Shocked, amazed
:- |	:-[	sarcastic

The young population of Internet and mobile phone users are quite adaptable to coining new words and inventing abbreviations and acronyms. Anyone who is new to this mode of communication may feel uneasy while tracing the underlying meaning of such lexical units. The dollar sign sometimes replaces 's', as in Micro$oft, and the pound sign may replace 'l', as in Ao£. Teenage users, in particular, have introduced several deviant spellings, such as 'kool' (cool) and 'fone' (phone). They replace a lower case 'o' with a zero, as in D00dz (dudes) and l0zers (losers), or use a percentage sign, as in c%l (cool). The Internet language dictionary has thousands of definitions explaining the online world of business, technology and communication, including the largest collection of Internet acronyms and text messaging shorthand. It is a popular site that helps geeks decode even the most cryptic conversations.

The impact of information technology can be seen in all spheres of life. In particular, Internet language has a tremendous influence on the art of advertising as both have their roots in originality and creativity. Internet advertising, although still the new kid on the advertiser's block, is a growing industry. Advertising masters are the first

people to notice the changes in a language and to reflect these changes in their advertising messages. Tehelka, known for its investigative journalism, appeals through e-banner to the readers to have subscription for the newspaper. The banner has an attractive line: *"The truth @ 100 Rs a year"*.

The shape of commerce has changed for today's business owners. No longer is the success of a business completely reliant on word-of-mouth and persuasive print advertising. Today's savvy entrepreneurs understand that in order to be truly successful in today's competitive environment, it is absolutely essential to conduct comprehensive Internet marketing. The beauty of Internet marketing is its relatively precise targeting ability. For instance, if I am a music freak and you are a sports enthusiast and both of us happen to be on the same page of the same website at the same time, it is very possible that my screen will have an ad for a music product, while your screen will have an ad for a sports product. This is essentially possible because it is much easier to electronically 'track' the behaviour and navigation of users on the Internet and 'target' them with ads or messages that are relevant to their profile.[10] It would take enormous effort and money to reach certain targeted audiences with specific messages delivered in a particular way. The Internet bridges the gap between all audiences and levels the playing field for those interested in marketing their services and products. eBay, which was set up as an online flea market or garage sale, has become the world's largest online marketplace—a worldwide bazaar of individual buyers and sellers—and it has invented a new form of doing business. There are no shops, no booths, no displays, just a phone line and a computer screen. eBay ads are great. They get the point across with

great emphasis that eBay has everything under the sun: *"Whatever IT is, you can get IT on eBay: from the hot new item ... to the hard-to-find collectible ... to the brand new product at a great price"*.

The Internet has revolutionised the media industry just as eBay is revolutionising retailing. If a business involves a product or service spread across the globe or even within a region, Internet marketing can be effective in showcasing the product or service to discerning buyers. It is a strong integrated marketing

communication (IMC) tool with great sales potential. It is capable of supporting and enhancing other IMC activities and has become central to the effectiveness of the IMC programme. The Internet is interactive. Newspapers, magazines and other print forms, such as direct mail, can be delivered online and their e-stories will look just like print stories. Since the Internet delivers messages to audiences electronically and has the capability to present moving images, it also fits the broadcast description. Thus, the Internet blurs the distinction between print and broadcast.[11]

The massive proliferation of the Indian Internet user base is already resulting in significant growth in Internet advertising and electronic commerce. This rapid expansion has spurred businesses to devote larger portions of their marketing budgets to Internet advertising. India boasts of an ever-increasing user base, whose understanding of the Internet is on par with any advanced nation worldwide. The Web is indeed becoming a household name, especially amongst upwardly mobile Indians, a fact that holds tremendous promise for e-commerce activities. To attract eyeballs, now that every brand wants to have its online avatar and connect itself with its target group, some of these sites have become informative and entertaining with brand awareness

activities, customer services and even games, contests and music and ad download options. Times Shopping and Futurebazaar.com have made online shopping fun by ushering in the era of 'sit and shop' Internet marketing in India. With an increasing number of websites offering everything under the sun, we can explore markets beyond our town by just sitting before the computer.

Many Indian portals such as Travelguru.com, Shaadi.com and Monsterindia.com are attracting the attention of surfers and enhancing the value of online services and utilities. Whether it is buying a movie ticket, a book from an online store or planning a pilgrimage itinerary, everything is easier and time-efficient in online marketing.

Blogging has become a big thing in the last few years, and some of the biggest and best known weblogs attract the kind of traffic of which even big-name e-commerce sites would be jealous. Blogs are basically online journals or diaries, which are great for sharing information and ideas. Blogs are often more than just a way to communicate—they become a way to reflect on life or works of art or any other subject under the sun. Advertising is making its way through blogs and today's marketing gurus feel that blogs, used strategically, can not only generate revenue directly, but can also be an effective way to communicate with prospects and customers and sound a call to action. A blog can be

private, as in most cases, or it can be an innovative media for business purposes. Being an interactive medium, blogs are used either internally to enhance the communication and culture in a corporate house or externally for brand awareness, brand building or to execute effective public relations programmes.

With the growing popularity and size of the Internet, social networking through online communities has enabled people all over the world to interact with friends, families and business acquaintances. It has opened a portal to meeting people of the opposite sex and to set up adult sexual friendships. It also enables the sharing of files, photos and videos through social networking websites such as Myspace, YouTube, Orkut, Bebo, Facebook, Flickr, iFilm, and Blogger. Social networking and blogging are the latest attractions for the youth in India. All social networking websites in India offer a free social media platform for users to connect and interact with other like-minded people and create their own world of expression and creativity. bigadda and ibibo are some such sites and they offer a number of fun-filled activities for their members. These sites are an attractive and accepted medium for advertising because of their huge user base. Social media sites have a lot of information such as user profile data, which can be effectively used to rank users or target a specific set of users for advertising. These sites enjoy great traffic because they are updated regularly with fresh content.

Matrimonial ads serve as a facilitating process for arranged marriages in India. They are essentially dialogues between families, using the medium of newspapers, where the particulars of the individual to be married and the family are detailed along with their requirements. Let us now look at a few examples of matrimonial advertisements, which are typically Indian and appear in the Sunday editions of all leading newspapers. Matrimonial ads offer ample opportunities to people to hunt for a marital partner of their choice. Even a decade ago, matrimonial ads were quite simple, straightforward, to the point and readable. This matrimonial ad was issued ten years ago:

Wanted beautiful, educated, homely match for Maheshwari Doctor boy 32/172, tall, handsome, friendly, vegetarian, father central govt officer, mother housewife, younger brother studying abroad, sister married in reputed family. ONLY Maheshwari families with decent background need apply. Others please excuse. Write Box. No. NDBL 110007.

This advertisement is a good example of the trends and structure of language in matrimonial ads ten years ago. It tells us a lot about the prospective bridegroom and gives details about all his family members. It reflects the Indian psyche and the Indian notion that marriage is a union, not only of two individuals, but of two families.

India's social fabric has retained most of its characteristics in the face of the so-called winds of liberalisation that have been blowing in the last decade. Caste and family are still paramount in the marital search process and change, if any, in these important social considerations is negligible. But matrimonial language and its structure have changed with time and technology. The use of language in recent matrimonial ads reflects new technology like the Internet and people's acceptance of this new medium. Here are two examples of matrimonial ads from a recent Sunday edition of *The Times of India*:

Reqd V/F B'ful Pqlfd gal for H'sm IITIAN, Com Sc, 27, 5'7" 151 lbs, 12Lpa C&D No bar. Only H/S F'mly apply. Send BHP BOX MUM 117198k.

SM 4Def Offr's dgt 32/5'4" Plkg, Hly'edu, Wkg top MNC, Mglk, Also good at H/H Affairs. Seek only MUM Stld Br. boy Email-PGB@hotmail.com Box-MUM 305707K.

A friend from my college days is an avid reader of matrimonial advertisements and he helped me unravel this maze of intricate abbreviations and acronyms. This is the code he wrote out for me:

Reqd	Required	SM 4	Suitable match for
V/F	Very Fair	Def Offr's	Defence Officer's
B'ful	Beautiful	Dgt	Daughter
Pqlfd	Professionally qualified	Plkg	Pleasant looking
H'sm	Handsome	Hly'edu	Highly educated
C&D	Caste & Dowry	Mglk	Manglik
H/S	High Status	H/H	Household
B/H/P	Biodata/Horoscope/Photo	MUM Stld	Mumbai settled
		Br.	Brahmin

There are reasons why such abbreviations have become the reality of today's classified advertising. Firstly, they save a great deal of time and space, and secondly, they reduce the matrimonial advertising expenditure by reducing the size of message. The client has to pay more money for a long, wordy and repetitive message. This new model of matrimonial advertising offers the client the opportunity to save money and also serves the purpose with an innovative messaging style. The rates for matrimonial ads are high and advertising agencies charge according to the number of characters or words.

Short Message Service, or SMS, is the harbinger of a new communication revolution that has mesmerised people worldwide. Mobile phones open up new ways of professional and social interaction using SMS. SMS is fast, attractive and, now, practically free thanks to the attractive rates offered by competing mobile service providers. It is more private and, without being vocal, you

SMS. The new language. HUTCh

can type your message and communicate with ease. After speech, SMS is the most attractive function for people on their mobile phones. Newer technology like WAP (wireless application protocol) phones and their tiny screens have motivated a whole new genre of abbreviated language forms. These messages need to be read and understood without referring to dictionary, thesaurus or grammar book because the words and phrases used are not part of any lexicography and the structure of the sentences does not conform to any standard grammar. Shakespeare would have been confounded to see his immortal line rendered thus: 2 B R NT 2 B (To be or not to be).

Acronyms are no longer restricted to words and short phrases; they can cover entire sentences: 'AYSOS?' ('Are you stupid or something?'), 'CID' ('Consider it done'), 'CIO' ('Check it out'), 'GTG' ('Got to go'), 'WDYS?' ('What did you say?'), 'MMYT' ('Mail me your thoughts'). Users are aware of the information value of consonants as opposed to vowels: 'TXT' ('Text') and 'XLNT' ('Excellent'). Some are like rebuses, in that the sound value of the letter or numeral acts as a syllable of a word, or are combinations of rebus and the letter initial: 'B4N' ('Bye for now'), 'CYL' ('See you later'), 'L8R' ('later'). Multi-word sentences and sequences of response utterances, especially of a stereotypical kind, can be reduced to a sequence of initial letters: 'SWDYT?' ('So what do you think?'), 'BCBC' ('Beggars can't be choosers'), 'BTBT' ('Been there, done that'), 'YYSSW' ('Yeah, yeah, sure, sure, whatever'), 'HHOJ' ('Ha, ha, only joking').

SMS has changed the lifestyles and attitudes of many mobile phone users. If ever there was a modern, techno Cupid, it is that small screen on mobile handsets. Like Helen of Troy, it's a face that has launched a thousand 'relation-ships'. As SMS becomes the latest addiction among the upwardly mobile, it is being increasingly used as an instant and intimate means of communication. The evidence is all around us.

If i tell u tht u hv a beutful bdy, wl u hld it agnst me?
Thr r so mny rsons to yearn for u. Luv is jst 1 of thm.

An MMS is wrth a thsnd txt mssgs.

Everywhere, at parties, clubs, restaurants, even on the streets, it's impossible to avoid the buzzing and clicking as people send or receive SMSes.[12] SMS helps even in healing broken hearts and broken friendships. Here is an excerpt from The Times of India, which highlights the beauty and utility of an SMS in bridging the gap between husband and wife:

> Diwali apart, I have fallen in love with the SMS, after a friend of mine let me in on his secret. He told me that it's SMS that comes to the rescue after his wife and he have had a serious quarrel. Not being on talking terms, they cannot communicate with each other, either at home or office. So they resort to indirect and succinct SMS messages on their cell phones. 'I M SoRI', he ends up writing, and 'IM2', she responds. Immediately he hops into his car to race back home for a longish lunch break. SMS has proved excellent as a facilitator.

So, all a couple needs is a couple of mobile phones with SMS facility to indulge in the fun of quarrelling—and then making up—as often as they like.

MMS mks SMS hstry.

But now even SMS is being replaced by the Multimedia Messaging Service, or MMS. With MMS, users can add life to their messages by adding photo, sound, colour, voice and animation. BPL Mobile, in the ad for its MMS service, shows a short message ('*dad, tell mom i hve fnd prfct bahu 4 her*') with the visual of a young, sensuous girl, who is the 'perfect bahu'. In another ad for MMS, a handsome executive sends a short message, '*stuk in jam*', with a visual of himself surrounded by four gorgeous young women as the probable reason for his being delayed. Mobile phones, with their tiny screens, have thrown up a whole new genre of abbreviated forms. Mobile phone users display a great deal of linguistic innovation and ingenuity in their messages.

Language is always studied in the context of society and the people who use it. The Internet has influenced all spheres of life to a great extent, and language, which is the heart of the Internet, is also taking new shape. There is no comparing Internet language with standard language. But with all its differences, this new medium seems to be distinct and genuine.

Notes

1. Naughton, John, 1999. *A Brief History of the Future: The Origin of the Internet* London: Weidenfeld & Nicolson, pp. 21–2.
2. Ibid., p.150.
3. Berners-Lee, Tim, 1999. *Weaving the Web.* London: Orion Business Books.
4. Crystal, David, 2000. *Language and the Internet.* Cambridge: Cambridge University Press, p. 10.
5. Chandra, N.D.R., 2003. 'Glocalisation of English in the Cyber Age: An Inter-linguistic Perspective', in *University News.* 41 (12), Mar 24–30, p. 2.
6. Crystal, David, 2000. *Languages and the Internet.* Cambridge: Cambridge University Press, p. 18.
7. Baron, Naomi S., 2000. *Alphabet to Email.* London: Rantledge, p. 248.
8. Crystal, David, 2000. *Languages and the Internet.* Cambridge: Cambridge University Press, p. 19.
9. Ibid., p. 22.
10. Tiwari, Sanjay, 2003. *The (Un)common Sense of Advertising: Getting the Basics Right.* New Delhi: Response Books, p. 23.
11. Wells, William, John Burnett and Sandra Moriarty, 2003. *Advertising: Principles and Practice.* New Delhi: Pearson Education Inc., p. 271.
12. Vasudev, Shefalee, 2002. 'Love in the Time of SMS', in *India Today.* October 14.

Eight

English versus Hindi

A Brief Analysis of Advertisements

A man's command of the language is most important. Next to kissing, it's the most exciting form of communication man has evolved.

— Oren Arnold

All the chapters preceding this one are based on the different linguistic aspects of Indian advertisements. This work concentrates on Indian English advertisements, but there has been an upswing in Hindi advertising in recent years, which makes it necessary to examine it more closely. My study so far has revealed that advertising is a creative art, which seeks to mesmerise prospective consumers with a perfect combination of copy and visual. In advertising, the copywriter manipulates language and designs messages with a suitable visual to establish a powerful bond between the consumer and the product. So, advertising is the creation of effective communication between these two elements. Today's audiences are increasingly becoming visually rather than linguistically articulate. But the right words in the right advertisements are still important.

Copywriting is a key activity in advertising, whether in Hindi or English. A copywriter translates the selling points of a client's product or services into benefits for selected consumers. He is concerned with what to say and show in an ad, and how best to say and show it. He is called upon to utilise all his creative talent to present those product benefits that best appeal to consumers. However, copywriting creativity is not pure, as is the work of a poet, novelist or playwright. It is a disciplined creativity, as rightly termed by a well-known author, it is not pure freedom of imagination. Certain checks are imposed on self-expression, so essential for any creative art. An ad copywriter writes with the purpose of achieving his client's objectives, rather than his own. What I am going to examine in this chapter is how English and Hindi advertisements differ at the copywriting level. In my study, I have noticed that English advertising deviates from Hindi advertising in terms of certain parameters. The subtleties of these two forms of advertising are the subject of study and analysis here.

Technology and the globalisation of economies have brought the world closer and turned it into one large marketplace. Advertisers and marketers sell products to consumers in different cultures and languages. To be successful in the international market, they need to communicate effectively with those target consumers. Therefore, much emphasis has been placed on the importance of intercultural communication, in which every language has a unique position and a specific audience set. According to my study, Hindi ads are less informative than English ads. But the two languages are similar in their use of creative strategy and technology. Being a global medium, English has a natural edge over Hindi as it goes beyond the borders of country and culture, delivering information to potential consumers worldwide. In the Indian advertising industry, these languages serve two main purposes—standardisation of the message and localisation of the international message in Hindi or any other vernacular language of the country. Standardisation stems from the view that people around the world share the same basic needs and values. The practitioners of standardisation believe that the same product can be advertised everywhere with the same or similar message and appeal. The opponents of standardisation argue that this is inappropriate because of the cultural and national differences among countries. They suggest that cultural differences should influence advertising practices and that advertising should be in local languages and designed to fit local markets.

Advertising in English is more experimental, investigative and bold, while advertising in Hindi seems to be plain in language, direct in presentation and easy to understand. English is the most widely spoken language in the world. It is a favourite medium because of its immense popularity and worldwide acceptance. English advertising has the upper hand over Hindi advertising. Being the international language of commerce and diplomacy, it allows advertisers and marketers to exploit its vast richness and wide network.

Nevertheless, advertising agencies started changing their strategy in the 1990s. In their aim to reach the maximum number of people, ad agencies started venturing towards creative campaigns that would take their clients' products to consumers in their own language. In the 1990s, creative directors became more serious over the issue of selecting the right medium for their products. Admen were quick to realise that Hindi was an equally strong medium of communication to reach the masses and sell their products. Although Hindi is recognised as India's national language and although it knits together different groups of people with different mother tongues, Hindi has never enjoyed much success in the past. Even its adoption as the country's national language sent a ripple of resentment through Southern India.

However, now, Hindi seems to be fitting in slowly with the requirement of today's generation and market. The language is increasingly taking its place in India, striding apace with globalisation and the media revolution in the country. The increasing desirability of Hindi can be traced to its ability to sell to a larger audience. From the morning cup of tea (*'Chai Ho To Aisi'*) to hoardings (*'Mujhme Hai Woh Baat'*), from SMS messages (*'Aati Kya?'*) to TV commercials (*'Thanda Matlab Coca-Cola'*), from Hindi greeting cards to children's cartoons and full-page ads in English publications that have slogans in Roman Hindi, from Hindi classes in finishing schools to Hindi folk songs blaring in the discos, there is an entire Hindustan thriving out there.[1]

When Hindi news channels went 24-hour, MTV turned *desi* and Hindi serials became a bedtime ritual in practically every second Indian household, no one realised that the erstwhile language of the *behenjis* and *bhaiyas* had donned a new, hip avatar. The Hindi news channel, Aaj Tak, is amongst the most popular news channel in the country today and its claim that it has changed the way news is delivered to Indian audiences is extremely credible. Aaj Tak has proved that a television anchor can reach all sections of society more effectively if he uses simple language than if he speaks like a pundit.

Gone are the days when advertisers would think a particular brand fit for English newspapers, and not Hindi papers. Today, Hindi and other regional newspapers hold as much importance in the media plan for any brand, especially as the Hindi newspaper business has grown in terms of both readership and advertising revenue. Even brands such as Mercedes Benz are advertised in Hindi newspapers now. The image of the Hindi speaking person, too, is changing. It is no longer associated with those who wear saris and dhotis. The social elite today accepts that Hindi is a *'lift kara de'* language. The Hindi-speaking political brigade, which includes Mulayam Singh Yadav, Mayawati and Lalu Prasad, has exploited this non-*firangi* language to connect with their vote base and move closer to the *aam aadmi*.

Amul butter was among the first few brands to realise the vast potential of Hindi advertising. Amul regularly launches effective and humorous Hindi advertising campaigns pegged on topical events. In the process, it has redefined the whole art of copywriting. Amul effectively broke the myth that any advertising message that does not use English is a failure. Here are some Amul ads:

Some ads are written exclusively in English like the one for Wills cigarettes. Being experimental and innovative in form, English advertising sometimes goes beyond good taste and borders upon obscenity and rudeness. Some ads display provocative and

erotic visuals, and the accompanying messages are derogatory and offensive in tone. This aspect of English advertising is more noticeable in ads for inner wear, contraceptives and aphrodisiacs, as I mentioned in the preceding chapters. One such television ad for Rupa inner wear tells the consumer: *'Prepare to Get Assaulted'*. In this television ad, the male model is shown accidentally entering a women's restroom and so irresistible is his inner wear that he is assaulted by the women inside. English copywriters make their statement baldly, as, for example, in the ad for MTV's music countdown show, which is termed *'the Baap of all Countdown Shows'*. The Feast ice cream ad associates the 'f' word openly for the first time with females.

Generally, ads for contraceptives and aphrodisiacs are designed in English. English ads are bolder and more sexually explicit. In most ads for contraceptives, 'the pleasure of making love' is the most perceptible theme. And these ads are growing increasingly more vocal and visible in depicting lovemaking, rather than talking about family planning, HIV/AIDS awareness and unsafe pregnancies. The body copy often takes on from the headline to explain the act of sex further in unabashed terms. Take this ad for Kohinoor condoms, for example.

Introducing Kohinoor Xtra Time Condoms. A new condom with a specifically formulated lubricant* to help you go on and on. So whenever you need to prolong that moment, ask for Kohinoor Xtra Time.

Kohinoor XTRA TIME
Ignite the Passion

In an ad for KamaSutra condoms, an attractive woman walks into a clinic. As she awaits her turn, she unzips the front pocket of the tote bag on her lap and starts to fiddle around in it. The man next to her notices her hand move suggestively. Then follows a male voiceover: *"So, what are you thinking of?"* A sly grin spreads across the man's face. The screen splits into two as a pack shot of KamaSutra condoms comes into view.

These ads have their Hindi versions, but they represent the social mores of society and maintain some levels of decency in communicating the brand message.

Nevertheless, even Hindi media is opening up to the expectations of the younger generation and we see some equally aggressive and sensual messages in Hindi advertising, as in the tagline for Zaroor condoms: '*Kaun Jane Kab Kahan Aur Kis Se Dil Ki Chahat Poori Ho Jaye.*'

One remarkable feature of the print media is that while ads may be in Hindi, the name and other details of the product will be in English. The language of packaging is English as we see in various ads in the print media. Certain ads have their entire copy in Hindi, but their taglines, indicating their brand, appear in English. The Hindi ad for Raymond, for example, has its baseline only in English.

Raymond

The Complete Man

In terms of selection of media and location, few ads have a permanent specific placement on a certain page in a magazine or newspaper. The exceptions include Bajaj Auto, which features its products regularly on the last page of the English edition of India Today, and Gold Flake, the ads of which usually appear on the second last page of the same magazine.

The art of translation is a valuable skill for an accomplished copy writer. Translation work is a vital activity in the advertising business. In a multilingual country like India, the possibilities of communicating a selling idea into several languages become easy and effective through translation. Translating consists of reproducing in the receptor language the closest natural equivalent of the source language message, first in terms of meaning, and second, in terms of style. But to reproduce the message, one must make a good many grammatical and lexical adjustments. Some Hindi ads have fresh copy written for them, but others are simply translations of their English versions. We have here some examples that reflect the significance of translation in advertising communication:

LIC: '*Hum Jaane Bharat Ko Behtar*' ('We Know India Better')

Philips: '*Aao Banaye Ek Behtar Kal*' ('Let's Make Things Better')

Indian Army: '*Hai Aap Mein Woh Josh, Woh Junoon?*' ('Do You Have It In You?')

Some translations are purely verbal and some are in the context of the messages. Since words cover areas of meaning and the semantic areas of corresponding words are not identical in different languages, it is inevitable that the choice of the right word in the receptor language to translate a word in the source language text depends more on the context than upon a fixed system of verbal consistency.

Hinglish, a mix of Hindi and English, is becoming increasingly popular in advertising communication. This is termed as code mixing. Advertising in Hinglish is fascinating and delightful. The popularity of the medium is obvious as the emerging middle class Indian is well versed in both languages. It suits both the market and the people equally. Words of both languages are being written in the Roman script as well as in the Devnagri script. I have cited many such ads in my earlier chapters. Here are some more examples:

Sprite: '*All Taste, No Gyaan*'

Domino's: '*Hungry Kya?*'

Bournvita: '*Confidence Kuch Kar Dikhaane Ka*'

Nature Fresh refined oil: '*Khao Light, Jiyo Light*'

Zandu Pancharisht: '*Hajma Fit Sehat Superhit*'

Hamdard Sualin: '*Asar Dikhaye, Naturally*'

Zandu: '*Pet Me Pollution, Nityam Churna Hi Solution*'

NECC: '*Sunday Ho Ya Monday, Roz Khao Ande*'

It is boom time for Hindi copywriters and advertising professionals because all global brands want local flavour and local language in India. This is a recognition of the fact that to stay in

MIND YOUR LANGUAGE

Like human beings, languages need to adapt to survive and flourish. That accounts for the phenomenal success of English. English has borrowed words like 'bazaar' and 'dharna' from Hindi and 'salon' and 'chic' from French, and these are just a few of its borrowed words.

"Language is an organism that breathes and grows. If you don't allow it to breathe, it will die. It has to embrace change to survive," says adman Prasoon Joshi.

Mrinal Pande, author and editor of the Hindi daily, *Hindustan*, agrees that Hindi needs to adapt to survive. She says it is happening right now. "Hindi dialects are finding place in the mainstream. You have Deccan Hindi, Gujarati Hindi and Bambaiya Hindi entering the mainstream."

Professor Sudhish Pachauri, who heads the Department of Hindi at Delhi University, believes there is nothing wrong if Hindi borrows English words to survive. "What do we lose if Hindi takes in 1,000 or 2,000 words from English?" he asks.

But at the same time, cautions Joshi, those who experiment with language should have a thorough knowledge of it in the first place. That ensures that the language doesn't lose its core sanctity. "Language has to fly. But it should not fly like a bird, but like a kite whose string is in the hands of a knowledgeable person," he says.

Source: Hindustan Times.

the Indian market, multinationals need to use a language that overcomes linguistic barriers and cultural differences. Priti Nair Chakravarthy, executive creative director, Lowe, is quite upfront in saying that she favours Hindi. She says, "Hindi rocks because it has the capacity to touch the pulse of the nation. When one uses Hindi or any other local lingo, one can add a lot more insight that is intrinsically Indian." She cites an interesting example: "'Enjoy Coca-Cola' is insipid when compared to 'Thanda Matlab Coca-Cola'."

Ad guru Prasoon Joshi explains why he supports Hindi vis-à-vis English: "Attitudes are best expressed in Hindi as people understand and immediately connect with the language. Hindi is our street language and it delivers the punch that is required when communicating with the masses. In comparison, English, for most

of us, is still a formal language. It is not a street language, like it is in New York."[2]

As the national language of India, Hindi not only serves the purpose of advertising, but also keeps the national fabric of the country in mind while doing so and devises strategies that reflect the spirit of the nation and its people. The following ad carries the message along with the Indian spirit of unity in diversity:

Hindu Muslim Sikh Isaai

Polio Rog Mitao Bhai

When a product or service is meant for the rural masses, English advertising fails to achieve the purpose of effective communication. This is where the role and importance of vernacular advertising come in. Vernacular advertising helps in reaching people with the right message. Hindi advertising is the best carrier, for example, to promote government policies, decisions and achievements. Ad campaigns for HIV/AIDS and polio raise greater awareness among rural people if they are communicated in their own language.

AIDS Ki Baat Sabke Saath

AIDS Ka Virodh Bas Ek Nirodh

The language of both the above lines is simple, clear and comprehensible to everyone. They generate better understanding among the masses. English advertising is too urban and sophisticated in such a setting and it cannot be equally successful in promoting all products and services in the country. There is no doubt that it appeals to a large number of people in India, but it is not necessary that it be an appropriate vehicle of communication to everyone all the time.

The headline is the most crucial part of an advertisement. Basically, it is used to arrest attention and create interest. I find English headlines more catchy and stylish than Hindi headlines. There are a number of words that recur frequently in effective headlines: 'New', "Quick', 'Why', "Important', 'Development', 'Announcing', 'Presenting', 'How To', 'Advice', 'Now', 'Easy', and 'The Truth About'.

Hindi headlines also have some frequently used words: 'Sarvapratham', 'Bharat Mein Pehli Baar', 'Bemisaal', 'Anokha', 'Adwitiya', 'Bejod', 'Bharpoor', 'Kifayati', and 'Beshkeemati'.

It is rather naive to think that the effectiveness of headlines comes from these specific words. Effectiveness comes primarily from content and only secondarily from the exact words used. If we have something new and sensational to advertise, then we can use these words in the headline. They are not—as some people maintain—hackneyed and tired. Newness and innovation are what attract attention, rather than specific words. 'How Women over 35 Can Look Younger' is the headline of an ad for a hormone cream, which women will understandably grant a second glance. 'Why Short Men Live Longer' is of wide interest to both short and tall men. Headlines that begin with these words invite further reading.

The fundamentals of advertising art are more or less consistent, irrespective of the language in which the ads are written. English advertising seems to be informative and research based. As we know, the most essential thing in any advertising campaign is to attract the consumer, stimulate his interest and invite him to buy the product. It is the magic of effective ad copy

---

Why We're Still Learning English

Hindi may be becoming more and more acceptable, but it still has a long, long way to go before it gains the kind of clout English enjoys. That is because just knowledge of Hindi is never good enough for the upwardly mobile Indian; knowledge of English is still regarded as essential.

"English still remains a language people aspire to speak because it remains the language of the powerful," explains Ashutosh, managing editor of Hindi news channel IBN 7.

"The attraction of English is still very strong. You will find that people in small towns and villages still lay a lot of stress on learning English. English is the language of aspiration, Hindi is the language of society," agrees Ravish Kumar, features editor, NDTV India.

Thanks to a colonial hangover, we have always been partial to English, which has given us an edge over many countries and is responsible for us bagging a major chunk of the lucrative global EPO business. This is why many feel that India shouldn't fiddle with a winning formula.

"Even China forces its people to speak English, but we don't have to do that," says Cyrus Oshidar, chief executive officer of brand solutions and youth marketing firm Bawa Broadcasting. "We will always be a dual culture. Ultimately, when we play on the global stage, it is an advantage to be a bicultural and bilingual society."

But will there come a time when the corporate world will embrace Hindi as the language of communication?

Adman Prasoon Joshi, who has noticed that in the boardroom, corporates switch in and out of Hindi more than they used to, says a complete switchover is unlikely for two reasons: (a) English is the international language of business, and (b) Hindi is a tech unfriendly language.

Source: Hindustan Times.

---

that transforms an ordinary reader into a potential buyer. Copywriters of both Hindi and English advertisements take liberties with the language and violate certain standard norms in order to be different and unique. By employing linguistic unorthodoxies, copywriters not only expand the 'flight of fancy', but also catch the attention of the reader. Still, Hindi advertising is new and budding with the linguistic gimmicks and 'forced incongruities' usually found in English advertising. In fact, Hindi advertising is simple, decent and to some extent reticent about the excessive linguistic variations and use of figures of speech. In fact, this pro-English slant is so high that it accounts for the puzzling contradiction that though Hindi TV channels and Hindi newspapers reach out to many lakhs more people than their English counterparts, the English media earns higher revenue because premium advertisers always choose English over Hindi.[4]

Graphological deviations are quite common in English advertising. Copywriters use the device effectively by changing the spelling of a word without affecting its pronunciation. They thus take advantage of homophony to promote a product: *'Gifts 4 U'* (Donear Fabrics) and *'Xtra Premium'* and *'Hi-Octane Petrol'* (Indian Oil Corp.).

These variations are used in the brand name or anywhere in the body copy of the advertisement. Another attractive instance of graphological variation is seen in the Amul butter ads. When Boris Becker lost to Mike Stick in the Wimbledon finals, the Amul ad employed both the proper nouns thus:

Stick to
the Winner
Amul
Baki Sab Bekar Hai

'Stick' is used as a verb and *'Bekar*, or Becker' as an adjective (Hindi). Phonological deviations are rarely noticed in English and Hindi advertisements. During my study, I found just one ad, that of Asian Paints, which has 'missus' pronounced as 'missej', a deviation from the standard pronunciation,/ˈmisiz/.

Grammatical and lexical violations abound in Hindi and English advertisements. I find the free use of disjunctive grammar in which minor and non-finite clauses are interdependent. Sentences very often do not have finite predicators and normally consist of only a nominal or adverbial group, which may consist of just one word. A few examples:

Yahoo:	*'Do you ... Yahoo?'*
Hyundai:	*'The Smarter Choice'*
Duracell batteries:	*'No Battery is Stronger, Longer'*
Onida:	*'Ever Seen a Television like This?'*
IBM (Think Pad):	*'I Think, Therefore IBM'*
BB&T:	*'There's Opportunity Here'*
Eureka Forbes:	*'Your Friend For Life'*
Johnson & Johnson:	*'Aur Aapka Sparsh, Saware Uska Kal'*

Jeeva Ayurvedic Soap: '*27 Ayurvedic Rahasya Jawan Jawan Si Komal Tvacha Ke Liye*'

Lexical violations and semantic deviations are the two most frequently used tricks in advertising language. These practices are easily seen in both English and Hindi advertising. Neologism is also a good way to create linguistic creativity and innovation in advertisements. Copywriters do not hesitate to break the boundaries of rules and coin new words and widen the possibilities of expression. For example, a new verb—'re-everythinged'—is coined and also prefixed and suffixed in the Volkswagen print ad.[4] This unusual aspect of language is an interesting feature of advertising messages.

re-tuned. re-conditioned. heck, it's been re-everythinged.

The National Egg Coordination Committee (NECC), in its promotion for eggs, says: '*Try an Eggsperiment*'. The NECC invites 'eggetarians' to eat more eggs because it says eggs are the most exciting way to get your daily dose of essential vitamins. Pepsi, in its recent campaign, appeals to young folks in a way with which they can identify: '*Yeh Hai Youngistaan Meri Jaan*'. It even coins a new term, 'Youngistaan', to position itself as a youth brand in order to garner a good market share in India.

Compounding is another productive technique in advertising language. This technique combines some parts of speech with another: '*wetlook*' (adjective + noun) or '*womanpower*' (noun + noun). Pre-modifiers, made up of noun + past participle, are also found regularly in advertising language, as, for example, '*sun-kissed beaches*' and '*moonlit drives*'. Many words are switched from Hindi to English and vice versa in advertising language. The code-switched nouns usually undergo slight changes in order to indicate number. For instance, '*joota*', the Hindi word for shoe, becomes '*jootas*', rather than '*joote*', which is the Hindi plural for shoes.

Indian words take a plural morpheme, as in sadhu/sadhus and rishi/rishis. A few words that have Sanskrit roots are transformed thus: *sutra/sutras* and *shastra/shastras*.

Some adjectives of quality are switched from Hindi to English to modify nouns: '*nayi*' (new) bike and 'pukka' (concrete) house.

To form the past tense, verbs take either the English inflectional suffix, '-d' or '-ed', as, for example, *gherao/gheraoed*. There are also many mixed words, in which English prefixes are attached to Hindi root words, such as '*super chai*' and '*grand mela*'.

Sometimes, Hindi or English suffixes are attached to each other, as in '*paperwala*', '*sadhuhood*' and '*cablewala*'.

Semantic variations are introduced in advertising language mainly by unequalled comparatives, illogicality of expression and role borrowing. These deviations can be seen in Hindi and English advertisements. The ad for Samsung refrigerators has a line: '*Keeps Food Fresher, Longer*'. We may ask the question, 'Fresher, longer than what?' We might not get an answer.

Role borrowing is a popular device in which registers of different linguistic roles are juxtaposed and often blended to create an impression. The ads for Aaj Tak, the Hindi news channel, often exercise this device by introducing a scene of a film shoot, an anecdote from the *Mahabharata* or a trial scene in a court room. The advertisement creators cleverly borrow the registers of a particular situation and merge them successfully with the selling idea of the product. This Amul ad banks heavily on role borrowing:

> *Stable ruler*
> *Even if it's hung*
> *Amul Butter*
> *Welcome Khaolition*

Homophony, homonymy and polysemy, of course, are the basis of a lot of wordplay, particularly for drawing the attention of the target audience. They are the most common kinds of ambiguities found in advertising language. These terms are liberally practised by copywriters to create puns in headlines or in body copy. An ad for the New York Stock Exchange employs a striking pun in its tagline: *The World Puts Its Stock in US.* (NYSE). The word, 'US', is a pun here intended to cause lexical ambiguity because it has two different messages: either people invest in the US (the United States) or they invest with our (us) stock exchange, i.e., the New York Stock Exchange. Here is another ad that plays with words and generates thrill and doubt at the same time: *The Best Things in the World Aren't Free. Just Duty Free.* (Chivas Regal).

As I said earlier, advertising is the art of mesmerising people. Besides these variations, there are many other formulas that are employed by copywriters to beguile readers into believing what they prescribe is the right choice. There are innumerable ads that reflect the copywriters' knowledge of rhetorical devices. Copywriters exercise the power of figures of speech in writing attractive headlines and catchy slogans. Some Hindi and English advertisements are the finest products of figurative language.

Metaphors and similes are commonly found in both forms of advertising. They are used to make a difference or comparison (simile) between the products and prove why their product is the leader (metaphor) in the market. A Hamdard Rogan Badam Shirin ad says: *'Sehat Ki Sanjivini'*, with 'sanjivini' being used as a metaphor.

These devices are important because of their emotive association with the products. Coca-Cola uses a simile in its tagline: 'Life Ho To Aisi'. The ad for the Bajaj Pulsar DTSi pushes the motorbike's robust, manly features thus:

Heads Will Turn
Hearts Will Miss Beats
Roads Will Burn

Introducing Digital Biking
Bajaj Pulsar DTSi
Definitely Male

This ad combines many rhetorical devices, such as personification, simile and metaphor in its body text.

Personification, in which an inanimate object is brought to life, is widely practised in both forms of advertising. Copywriters endow a product with human qualities, emotions and activities so that it will be associated closely and impressively with the user. Some examples:

GE:	*'Imagination at Work'*
TVS Victor:	*'More Smiles/Hour'*
Asian Paints:	*'Har Ghar Kuch Kehta Hai'*
Sunsilk:	*'Jagao Apne Balon Ko'*
United Airlines:	*'Fly the Friendly Skies'*

Allusion is another striking figure of speech equally exploited by copywriters. This consists of some words or expressions which refer to some well-known incident in the past or a mythical or historical name or a prominent person's words. Many hotels in India take their names from the country's rich heritage, as, for example, Maurya Sheraton and Taj Mahal Hotel. Other examples of this device are Lal Quila basmati rice, Taj Mahal tea, Charminar cigarettes and Tiranga gutkha. Such names add an aura of grandeur and nobility to the product and consumers feel elevated while using brands bearing such names.

Copywriters are also fond of using alliteration and rhyme and these are found abundantly in Hindi and English advertisements. Effective employment of these devices makes ads more musical, memorable and appealing. Here are some examples:

Chevrolet:	*'Eye It, Try It, Buy It'*
Ministry of Water Resources:	*Jal Jodo Jan Jodo,*
	Jan Jodo Man Jodo'
Kurkure:	*'Chai Shai Mast Ho Jaye'*

Hyperbole and euphemisms are other popular figures of speech commonly noticed in advertising language. Exaggeration is a statement or description that makes something seem larger, better, worse or more important than it really is. It is employed to catch the attention of the consumer and to highlight the product. Euphemisms are indirect words or phrases that advertisers use to refer to something embarrassing or unpleasant, sometimes to make it seem more acceptable than it really is. Some examples are:

Reliance Mobile:	*'Kar Lo Duniya Mutthi Mein!'* (exaggeration)
Coca-Cola:	*'Things Go Better with Coke'* (exaggeration)
Surf Ultra:	*'Daag Dhoondte Reh Jaoge'* (exaggeration)
Baidyanath Sundari Kalp:	*'Aasan Banaye Un Kathin Dinon Ko'* (euphemism)

There are some delightful English ads which make use of the *Bible*. The ads are written in such a way that they look similar to biblical utterances. For example:

Amul butter:	*'Give Us This Day Our Daily Bread with Amul Butter'*
Life Insurance Corp. of India:	*'Trust, Thy Name is LIC'*

Similarly, some Hindi advertising slogans are chanted like Sanskrit shlokas, as in the TV ad for Vim bar.

If print had music, it would be typography. Typefaces are decoded as we read the message. The cut of each letter transmits dozens of signals to the brain. Typography underscores words with emotional presence, creates atmosphere, and colours the way we want our messages interpreted.[6] Typographical ads can communicate ideas which cannot be expressed in traditional ways. The ad for J&B Scotch whisky, which is based on typography, is very simple and inspiring and drives the brand idea perfectly. In the ad, J&B associates itself beautifully with the holiday season and the ensuing celebrations and shows, through a distinct

typeface, that the concept of fun and cheer—(J)ingle (B)ells, (J)ingle (B)ells—is incomplete without J&B: 'The Holidays Aren't the Same Without J&B'.

A well-chosen typeface can give a unique identity to a product and turn low-budget print ads into highly visible, cutting edge ads. It helps in shaping the personality of a brand. Legibility should be the prime concern while choosing a typeface. It shouldn't be a forced move to introduce a new idea with the brand. It should be effortless, seamless and in complete harmony with the ad copy.

Language is a forceful, appropriate and permanent means of communication. Advertising language uses innumerable linguistic variations and rhetorical devices in its messages. Besides verbal communication, advertising language makes use of many non-linguistic symbols such as expressive body gestures, signals of various kinds, traffic lights, road signs, flags, emblems and mathematical symbols. They may be termed as means of communication, yet they are not as flexible, complete and meaningful as language. In my study, I came across many ads that use mathematical signs:

Dettol: Be 100% pure
Bajaj Caliber: ***** Rating: Hoodibaba!
Jockey: The Next Best Thing To | < | Naked

Wordless copy is a bright example of non-verbal communication in the world of advertising. At times, billboards carry merely an inscription, like the Amul ads, which are pictorial in form, but totally wordless apart from the single tagline. Air India and Amul have, perhaps, the greatest number of masterpieces to their credit in this genre through their billboards projections dating from the early 1950s.

The Internet has generated a new linguistic medium, which differs in some ways from traditional speech and writing. This Internet language is known by many names, as we have seen in an earlier chapter, and is quite distinct from standard language. It is this unique and unusual way of expressing oneself within different e-discourses that attracts advertising gurus to promote their brands through this medium. We witness an enormous amount of idiosyncrasy and variation in all e-encounters. Internet users are innovative and creative in their linguistic expressions in all Internet-mediated situations. Besides its linguistic versatility, the Internet offers an inexpensive, quick and easily available interactive medium. It is also a most flexible media and allows immediate change of messages in reaction to market and competitive conditions. Most Internet browsers use English as their medium of communication. English is accepted as the global medium for all Internet communication. While there are a few Hindi websites on the Internet, their contribution to overall Internet communication is paltry. So, Hindi advertising on the Internet is not worth taking up at present.

Previously, an almost Urduised Hindi had dominated our cultural space, including Bollywood, for years. But a trend that first started with advertising brought down that Hindi from its pedestal and made it more accessible and workable. Liberalisation meant that prosperity flowed into smaller towns such as Meerut, says Mrinal Pandey, author and editor of the Hindi daily, *Hindustan*.

"There is no market in India as big as the Hindi heartland. And when a market is big, it demands its language. The demand is, 'If you want to sell me your brand, sell it to me in my language'," says Professor Sudhish Pachuari, literary and media critic.[7] The footprint of the Hindi market is every marketer's dream. Other Indian languages represent one or two states, but Hindi and its dialects are the mother tongue in 11 states. Thus, not surprisingly, Hindi is where the revenue is.

Nevertheless, the importance of English has never diminished. The advent of the Internet and globalisation has only strengthened it. But the chemistry between English and Hindi has changed. Hindi no longer considers English an arch-rival. The two languages have come closer and they deliver perfectly when they work in tandem. The result is a truly winning blend, which has become a new mantra in social acceptance, prestige and success. Right from the Dabar Chyawanprash tagline, *'Banaye Andar Se Strong'* to Coca-Cola's *'Life Ho To Aisi'*, ad messages today are a unique blend of English and Hindi.

Notes

1. Vasudev, Shefalee. 2004. 'The Hindi High', in *India Today*. June 7. pp. 70-74.

2. Anand, Tuhina. 2005. June 6, 2007.
   www.agencyfaqs.com/news/stories/2005/10/13/ 12949.html
3. Braganza, Colleen. 2008. 'Yeh Dil Maange More', in *Brunch*,
   supplement of *Hindustan Times*. July 20. pp. 6-9.
4. Ibid.
5. Sells, Peter, and Sierra Gonzalez. January 24, 2006.
   www.stanford.edu/class/linguist34/Unit_07/ is_it_normal.htm
6. Aitchison, Jim. 2008. *Cutting Edge Advertising*. Singapore:
   Pearson Education South Asia. p. 274.
7. Braganza, Colleen. 2008. 'Yeh Dil Maange More', in *Brunch*,
   supplement of *Hindustan Times*. July 20. pp. 6-9.

Nine

Conclusion

IN ADVERTISING,
WHAT DO DETERGENTS
WASH BETTER: WHITE,
COLORS OR BRAINS ?

THERE'S NOTHING BAD ABOUT ADVERTISING AS LONG AS IT'S GOOD.

Language is a fundamental and important part of human behaviour in any society and the nature and structure of language is worth studying in its own right. We all speak and use language, but we tend to take it for granted rather like the environment that surrounds us—the atmosphere, the force of gravity and other natural phenomena. Language, however, is not a natural phenomenon; it is a creation of man's social needs. Like all other living creatures, we depend on the air, water and earth around us, and in the same way, society depends upon language for its very existence. Language and human culture are intimately related and the one is indispensable to the other. What is more, like society, language is constantly evolving and subject to growth and change in much the same way as a living organism.

Whether we are aware of it or not, one form of communication in which modern man is increasingly involved is advertising. I have concerned myself so far with the ways in which language modifies itself in tune with advertising communication. I have further investigated advertising language to unearth its linguistic creativity and playfulness, to dig out how it is possible for consumers to comprehend the 'potential linguistic googlies' bowled to them in advertising messages.

Advertising performs many basic roles. It mediates between the abstract and the concrete as well as between social values, cultural symbols and ordinary everyday consumerist culture. Further, it is a communication process and an intersection of at least two major types of communication—that of signs and of values. In other words, it uses the dialogue of signs to affect the exchange of values. We also see the two faces of advertising: a surface representation of ideas that is easy to understand, and a second, hidden level, which underlies the surface representation and endows it with meaning. Yet this 'other' meaning is not immediately clear and it needs decoding in various ways.

Whether ads are in English or Hindi, they touch zones in which we are vulnerable and make their appeals in terms of established meanings and values which have been validated in our experience or culture, or to those social and human aspirations which are not adequately expressed or fulfilled in modern life. Advertising acts as a saviour. It does this initially by highlighting the essential dilemmas of the human world and finally by offering a solution to these dilemmas. In buying a certain product or service, one buys not only a 'thing', but also an image. This image consists of the belief in and hope of something better.

Of all the modern ways of communication in which language is used, advertising is one of the most striking and one that arouses strong feelings. As I have pointed out in the first chapter of this book, language is a means of mass communication and it makes mass selling possible through advertisements. A baby crying for its feed, a girl seeking her Prince Charming, a housewife who desires a new sari—all these are aspects of advertising. They want to communicate, to persuade, to influence and to lead to some action.

Advertising is an effective communication between the producer and the consumer. To know what role language plays in making advertising communication more convincing and enduring, I have studied in depth the world of advertising today in the second chapter of this book. I have touched upon the various aspects of advertising, including a brief history of ads, types of ads, concepts of positioning, brand image and unique selling proposition, copywriting for different media, developing headlines and body copy in an ad and other issues. I have observed that as long as the selling idea fetches money, copywriters do not hesitate to bend the rules of the game and create a new lingo for their products' publicity.

Chapter 3 underlines the sociolinguistic base of advertisements. It studies the way in which language interacts with society. I have added the unique sociolinguistic setting of Arunachal Pradesh in this chapter. Arunachal Pradesh has a multilingual society, a fascinating conglomeration of tribes and sub-tribes, each with their own independent dialects and customs. Every tribal group is distinct with its own linguistic identity. They speak distinct dialects derived from the North Assam branch of the Tibeto-Burman sub-family of the Sino-Tibetan language stock. Every dialect is known by the name of its tribe. Though there are around twenty-five tribes speaking seventy dialects, the question of distinguishing language from dialects does not arise at this stage. None of the tribes have any script, except Khampti, which uses a variation of the Shan script. The Monpas use the Tibetan script for their religious scriptures. The state does not have its own regional language and, hence, the lack of a script for written communication. All the dialects seem to serve the purpose of speech communication, but due to the absence of an authentic script, the dialects do not deliver much in written form. Some tribal groups have adopted the Roman script for written communication, but this is not an exact measure. There are certain phonemes and paralinguistic features in the dialects, which cannot be communicated in the Roman script as it is practised in oral communication. With all its limitations, the Roman script helps the government machinery to deliver information about its policies and decisions and other such announcements to the people of Arunachal Pradesh. Granted the practical importance of writing, attempts are being made by researchers and local linguists to invent an original script for the society.

The second part of this chapter is about code switching. In the current Indian advertising scene, I have found code switching to be one of the most common practices for all types of advertisements. Hindi and English words are the main components of code switching. More and more English and Hindi words are seen in each other's ad copy. With globalisation coming to the fore, these two languages have developed a reciprocal bond that delivers the ultimate punch in advertising messages to attract the target audience and invite it to act and buy the advertised products. The third part of this chapter examines sexist language in advertisements. Sexual incitement is rarely absent from advertising. Almost every advertisement which appeals to sexuality ends up reducing women to the status of objects to be acquired and possessed by men. What is more, the advertisements imply that this is how women want to see themselves—as desirable and beautiful possessions.

Chapter 4 concentrates on the psychological variables that govern consumer behaviour in buying a product. Companies that want to understand how consumers think and make decisions about products conduct sophisticated consumer behaviour research to identify their consumers, why they buy, what they buy and how they buy. Besides culture and society, we have certain internal elements that make us individuals. The elements that shape our inner self are our psychological make-up. Although hundreds of different elements are encompassed under the term, 'psychological', the elements with the most relevance to advertising are perception, learning, motives, attitudes and lifestyles. In this chapter, I have divided advertisements as per the target audience: Ads for the family, for men of the 1980s and 1990s, for new men, for feminists, for children and ads with colour prejudice.

I have noticed that a new trend is emerging in advertisements, which highlights the changing values and attitudes of the new Indian male. This new man believes in equality of the sexes and does not take women for granted. At the same time, the ad world has created a new kind of female, who is sexist, abusive, insensitive, chauvinist and hormone driven. Some ads dictate that women's emancipation can only be seen in terms of a fair complexion, so a Fair & Lovely comes to the rescue of Indian women and ensures them a bright future by lightening their skin colour. Advertising gurus are quick to recognise the psychological weakness of human beings and deliver their promises accordingly. To some extent, advertising is a statement on the human psyche as well as the prevailing trends in society.

Lobov points out that the first and most important step is to distinguish 'what is said from what is done'—that discourse analysis must be concerned with the functional use of language. For the discourse analysis of ads, I have assessed the advertising discourse in terms of cohesion, coherence, the cooperative principle and the concept of schemata. It is noticed that some ads have a conversational implicature and, in order to comprehend them fully, we should have background knowledge of the conversation. It is equally important in discourse analysis to notice the deictic expression and presupposition that undertakes the intended meaning of the speaker. Chapter 5 discusses the value of pragmatic and semiotic units in advertisements. The study of the place and visual semiotics of advertisements is a significant feature of this chapter.

Chapter 6 studies how consumers respond to visual images and what implications that response has on the marketing of products. It adds a new dimension to this study, in which I explore the subtleties of visual images and develop the meaning conveyed in advertising messages. The production of meaning from advertising visual messages has been an extremely interesting and insightful experience for me. In order to investigate the production of meanings from visuals, I have selected some visually potential images from the world of advertising and attempted to read the different shades of meaning inherent in them as an exploratory effort for this study. Many print advertisements are reviewed and instances of linguistic manipulation are also identified and explained within visual images. Semiotics, the study of signs, which stems from the early work of Saussure and Pierce is the main source and inspiration for the conceptualisation of this chapter. The theories of these two masters can be applied to virtually any sign that signifies a meaning or concept as a means of communication in the outside world.

The Internet is one of the most important happenings of the last century. It has been a tremendous force in changing the way we communicate, work, trade, live and learn. It is reshaping national frontiers and overcoming cultural differences. It would be surprising indeed if such a radically innovative phenomenon did not have a corresponding impact on the way we communicate. In Chapter 7, I have examined the impact of the Internet on the traditional form of speech and writing. The Internet has offered us a genuine new medium that is catchy, intimate, informal and, to some extent, free from the clutches of grammar.

The distinctiveness of the Internet language is found largely in graphology and lexicon—the two levels of language where it is relatively easy to introduce innovation and deviation. An example of this is a signboard for a car remodelling service, which says: 'U GIV US UR CAR, V GIV U N XTENSIVE DESIGNER LUK'. We find many neologisms, phrases and expressions which display the uniqueness and novelty of the rapidly growing, computer-mediated communication. New jargon and netiquette are gaining ground. Internet language has introduced a whole new range of acronyms and abbreviations, which are equally popular in sending SMSes from one mobile phone to another as in classified advertisements. With their economy of word size and beauty of expression, many people use these abbreviations to save, time, space and, of course, money.

In order to be different and impressive, advertising communication can bring about any number of innovations in the existing pattern of language and its applications. Advertising language offers boundless scope for violation of the rules and conventions of language. As the poet takes liberties with language in order to enrich his expression, the copywriter widens and deepens the potentialities of language in several ways. Synthesis of conception, economy of expression, the lyricism that contributes to memorability—these skills that are so essential to good advertising are also the basic tools of the poet.

Chapter 8 brings out the differences between Hindi and English advertising and shows the prevailing trends in Indian advertising art. It talks of the 'cool quotient of Hindi' and how it has suddenly become the preferred choice of the younger generation and the market. This chapter is a kind of synthesis of the linguistic idiosyncrasies and variations seen in both Hindi and English advertisements. It highlights all the linguistic tricks and marketing gimmicks used by the copywriter to sell products in different media. The copywriter employs words that arouse the senses—the aromatic smell of a cigar, the seductive fragrance of a perfume, the lemon freshness of a bath soap, and the relaxation that comes from smoking a cigarette after a hard day's work.

Colours, too, have their own meaning in advertising. Blue connotes authority or masculinity. Purple stands for majesty or royalty. Orange, red and blue stand high on the attention-getting list. Colours play an important role because the purpose of advertising copy is to persuade consumers and to explore the most effective avenues of approach to his consciousness.

English advertising is more experimental, investigative and bold, while Hindi advertising is plain in diction, direct in presentation and easy to understand. Being innovative in form, English advertising sometimes touches low levels of obscenity and rudeness in its tone. Hindi advertising is still quite nationalist in its approach and maintains decency and simplicity in its messages.

Translation is another important key area in multilingual advertising. Hinglish is a popular mode of advertising communication. Linguistically, it is called code switching. English advertising is too urban and sophisticated in its setting and cannot be equally successful in promoting all products and services in a multilingual country like India. As the national language of the country, Hindi not only serves the purpose of advertising, but while doing so, keeps the national fabric of the country in mind and devises strategies that reflect the spirit of the nation and its people. It has deeper accessibility to the rural masses in the country. Both Hindi and English advertising employ different figures of speech: metaphor, simile, allusion, alliteration, rhyme, personification, hyperbole and euphemism. Hindi advertising also employs *shabda shakti* and *alankars*. An example of a tagline used in an election campaign:

Kiske Gale Padenge Haar

Kiske Gale Padegi Haar

Rasas are also a part of advertising messages. Besides verbal communication, advertising language relies also on mathematical symbols, road signs, traffic signals, body gestures and pictures.

Language empowers advertising messages. Advertising professionals are an imaginative bunch of people, who love to explore language. We also see the other side of this medium, in which language is mutilated and distorted for enhanced effect, rather than for effective communication. Language is a great tool for advertisers to use to communicate a clear idea. If they use language creatively, they can hear their brand talk directly to the consumers and create an embellished personality for their brand. Advertising messages are communicated through language, whether Hindi, English or any other, but the bottom line of using a particular language is to create an idea that is compelling, convincing and saleable. I feel that advertising techniques are changing fast, but the enduring principles of good communication remain the same. We all love fresh, interesting and intelligent ideas communicated with the utmost simplicity. Whether they are the international ads for the Volkswagen and Avis or our own desi Fevicol ads, they stand tall and connect easily to the audiences because of their innovative ideas and simple presentation. The Fevicol commercial is a pathfinder in the advertising industry and portrays its message successfully without a whisper or a word. No language is interchanged and all the characters are shown to be silent spectators. The commercial shows an unshakeable mountain of passengers aboard an overloaded truck in Rajasthan. The brand is Indian, the people are Indian, the moment is Indian, the colours are Indian, the sound is Indian, but it is understood with equal facility anywhere in the world

Any recommendation about the approach and style of advertising language seems to be like walking in the dark. It is difficult to develop a unified and common structure for advertising language—it flows like a stream and moves, swings and spreads into various tributaries, complementing the social environment, values and expectations. We cannot be definitive about its structure and application; the extraordinary persuasiveness it possesses and the magical charms it weaves are all beyond the standard norms of language. Advertising language is distinct and versatile and it should not be compared with standard language. It specialises in those features of language that we generally try to overcome as irregularities in our everyday communication. It banks heavily on linguistic oddities such as phonological and graphological deviations *('missej' instead of missus and 'U' instead of you)*, lexical and semantic violations *('Skinnocence' and 'Sabka Rub Ek')*, grammatical variations *(M-Seal—'Seals, Joins, Fixes, Builds')* and ambiguities. And I feel that is the hallmark of advertising language. Besides effective communication, commerce is at the heart of advertising. As long as the advertising message fetches money, copywriters won't think twice before playing with the vastness of language.

Appendices

I
The Linguistics of Logos: The HUL Logo Decoded

Every brand's logo represents what the company stands for. In the never-ending race to catch eyeballs, marketers have always tried to make their brand logos eye-catching and memorable. McDonald's Golden Arches and Coca-Cola's curvy logo figure among the five most recognised symbols in the world today. In India too, brand logos are becoming increasingly recognisable. Even a few years ago, the most commonly used symbols in Indian brands' logos were the sun, the tree and the elephant. This has changed with the advent of a number of design firms in the past few years. Hindustan Unilever Ltd (HUL), which was earlier known as Hindustan Lever Ltd, not only has a new name, but also a new logo. The thinking is that the new name provides an optimum balance between maintaining the heritage of the company and the synergies of the global alignment with the corporate name of Unilever. HUL's new logo is symbolic of the company's mission to add vitality to life. The logo comprises 25 different icons representing the organisation, its brands and the idea of vitality.

Sun: Our primary natural resource. All life begins with the sun, the ultimate symbol of vitality.

DNA: The double helix, the genetic blueprint of life and a symbol of bioscience. It is the key to a healthy life. The sun is the biggest ingredient of life, and DNA the smallest.

Bee: Represents creation, pollination, hard work and biodiversity. Bees symbolise both environmental challenges and opportunities.

Hand: A symbol of sensitivity, care and need. It represents both skin and touch.

Flower: Represents fragrance. When seen with the hand, it represents moisturisers or cream.

Hair: A symbol of beauty. Placed next to the flower, it evokes cleanliness and fragrance. Placed near the hand, it suggests softness.

Palm Tree: A nurtured resource. It produces palm oil as well as fruit, and is also a symbol of paradise.

Sauces or Spreads: Represent mixing or stirring. They also suggest blending in flavours and adding taste.

Spoon: A symbol of nutrition, taste and cooking.

Bowl: A bowl of delicious smelling food. It can also represent a ready meal, hot drink or soup.

Spice and Flavours: Represent chillies or fresh ingredients.

Fish: Represents food, sea or fresh water

Sparkle: Clean, healthy and sparkling with energy

Bird: A symbol of freedom. It suggests relief from daily chores and getting more out of life

Recycling: Part of HUL's commitment to sustainability

Lips: Represent beauty, looking good and great taste

Ice Cream: A well-deserved treat, pleasure and enjoyment

Tea: A plant or an extract of a plant. Also a symbol of growing and farming

Particles: Reference to science, bubbles and fizz

Frozen: The plant is a symbol of freshness, the snowflake represents freezing. So, this is a transformational symbol

Wave: Symbolises cleanliness, freshness and vigour

Liquid: A reference to clean water and purity

Container: Symbolises packaging—a pot of cream is associated with personal care

Clothes: Represents fresh laundry and looking good

Heart: A symbol of love, care and health

Source: The Brand Reporter, July 16–31, 2007, Vol. II, Issue 24.

II
SMS Lingo: A Linguistic Renaissance

Parents need no longer worry for a new study says that SMSes and online chats actually help teenagers hone their linguistic abilities, rather than degrade them. The parental worry has stemmed from the lack of grammar and the extensive use of often unintelligible abbreviations such as LOL, OMG and TTYL in SMSes, which is also known as instant messaging (IM). But the study has concluded that IM represents 'an expansive new linguistic renaissance' being evolved by GenNext kids. Researchers at the University of Toronto have pointed out that teenagers risk familial censure and the ridicule of friends if they use slang. But IM allows them to deploy a 'robust mix' of colloquial and formal language. They based their conclusions on an analysis of more than a million words of IM communication and a quarter of a million spoken words produced by 72 people aged between 15 and 20 years. The researchers argue that far from ruining teenagers' ability to communicate, IM lets teenagers show off what they can do with language.

"IM is interactive discourse among friends that is conducive to informal language," said Derek Denis, co-author of the study, "but at the same time, it is a written interface which tends to be more formal than speech." The researchers found that although IM shared some of the patterns used in speech, its vocabulary and grammar tended to be relatively conservative.

For example, when speaking, teenagers are more likely to use the phrase, "He was like, 'What's up?'" than "He said, 'What's up?'", but the opposite is true when they are instant messaging. This supports the idea that IM represents a hybrid form of communication.

Nor do teens use abbreviations as much as the stereotype suggests: 'LOL' ('Laugh Out Loud'), 'OMG' ('Oh My God') and 'TTYL' ('Talk to You Later') made up just 2.4 per cent of the vocabulary of IM conversations—an 'infinitesimally small' proportion, say the researchers. And rumours of the demise of the word 'you' would appear to have been greatly exaggerated: It was preferred to 'u' a whopping nine times out of ten.

In fact, the study suggests that the use of such short forms is confined mostly to the youngest users of IM. The findings of the study have been published in 2008 in the spring issue of the journal, *American Speech*.

Source: HindustanTimes.com

III
Common Words in Advertising

A study of the vocabulary used in advertising lists the most common adjectives and verbs in order of frequency. They are:

Adjectives		*Verbs*	
1.	new	1.	make
2.	good/better/best	2.	get
3.	free	3.	give
4.	fresh	4.	have
5.	delicious	5.	see
6.	full	6.	buy
7.	sure	7.	come
8.	clean	8.	go
9.	wonderful	9.	know
10.	special	10.	keep
11.	crisp	11.	look
12.	fine	12.	need
13.	big	13.	love
14.	great	14.	use
15.	real	15.	feel
16.	easy	16.	like
17.	bright	17.	choose
18.	extra	18.	take
19.	safe	19.	start
20.	rich	20.	taste

Good and **new** were more than twice as popular as any other adjective.

Source: http://www.linguarama.com

IV
Netlingo

Everyday, the Internet expands by the social, political, and economic activities of people all over the world, and its impact growth exponentially. The new technology, David Crystal says, is causing a "revolution" in human communication to rank alongside the advent of human speech itself. "So far we have been communicating in speech, writing and with sign language. But the internet is neither speech nor writing. It has aspects of both and represents a new form." In cyberspace actions and reactions are essentially instantaneous, and this is why the Internet is so gratifying and attractive.

afaik – as far as I know	f? – friends?
afk – away from keyboard	fotcl – falling off the chair laughing
asap – as soon as possible	f2f – face to face
a/s/l – age/sex/location	fwiw – for what it`s worth
atw – at the weekend	fya – for your amusement
awhfy – are we having fun yet?	fyi – for your information
bbfn – bye bye for now	g – grin
bbl – be back later	gal – get a life
bcnu – be seeing you	gd&r – grinning ducking and running
b4 – before	gmta – great minds at work
bfd – big fucking deal	gr8 – great
bg – big grin	gsoh – great sense of humour
brb – be right back	hhok – ha ha only kidding
btw – by the way	hth – hope this helps
cfc – call for comments	ianal – i`m not a lawyer but...
cfv – call for votes	icwum – I see what you mean
cm – call me	idk – I don`t know
cu – see you	iirc – if I don't remember correctly
cul – see u later	imho – in my humble opinion
cul8r – see you later	imi – I mean it
cya – see you	imnsho – in my not so humble opinion

dk – don't know

dur? – don't you remember

eod – end of discussion

irl – in real life

jam – just a minute

j4f – just for fun

jk – just kidding

kc – keep cool

khuf – know how you feel

l8r – later

lol – laughing out loud

m8 – mate

mtfbwu – may the force be with you

na – no access

nc – no comment

np – no problem

now – no way out

obtw – oh by the way

o4u – only for you

oic – oh I see

otoh – on the other hand

pmji – pardon my jumping in

ptmm – please tell me more

rip – rest in peace

rotf – rolling on the floor

rotfl – rolling on the floor laughing

rtm – read the manual

ruok – are you OK?

sc – stay cool

smote – sets my teeth on edge

so – significant other

sohf – sense of humour failure

sol – sooner or later

imo – in my opinion

iou – I owe you

iow – in other words

t+ – think positive

ta4n – that's all for now

tafn – that's all for now

thx – thanks

tia – thanks in advance

tmot – trust me on this

tnx – thanks

ttfn – ta ta for now

tttt – to tell the truth

t2ul – talk to you later

ttytt – to tell you the truth

tuvm – thank you very much

tx – thanks

tyvm – thank you very much

wadr – with all due respect

wb – welcome back

w4u – waiting for you

wrt – with respect to

wtfigo – what the fuck is going on?

Wu – what's up?

Wuwh – wish you were here

X! – typical women

Y! – typical man

Yiu – yes I understand

2bctnd – to be continued

2d4 – to die for

2g4u – too good for you

2l8 – too late

4e – forever

4yeo – for your eyes only

Source: Language and the Internet, D Crystal.

V
Amul: Utterly Butterly Forever

The Amul moppet has featured in hoardings for almost four decades, making the Amul campaign the longest running ad campaign in the world. The hoardings display one-liners that constitute a veritable commentary on contemporary political and social events, with a new theme being featured each week.

On the budget incorporating value added tax (VAT)

On the sensex reaching a new high

Property dispute between the Ambani brothers

Controversy on the cola brands containing pesticides

Jayalalitha and Mamta in the news

Emerging friendly relations with other countries like Israel

On Dr A.P.J. appointed President of India

On Dr Manmohan Singh being elected PM

VI
Some Cultural Words of Wisdom

All cultures phrase their teachings in brief, easy-to-remember sayings. A characteristic of such sayings is that they are made to appear true and appropriate for all times and for all situations. The absurdity becomes apparent when opposites are juxtaposed.

Two is company, three's a crowd :: The more the merrier

It never rains, but it pours :: Every cloud has a silver lining

A chain is only as strong as its weakest link :: In unity there is strength

Better late than never :: The early bird catches the worm

Jack of all trades, master of none :: If you want a thing done well, do it yourself

Out of sight, out of mind :: Absence makes the heart grow fonder

A bird in hand is worth two in the bush :: Nothing ventured, nothing gained

Rome wasn't built in a day :: Make hay while the sun shines

He who hesitates is lost :: Look before you leap

All work and no play makes Jack a dull boy :: Keep your nose to the grindstone

Too many cooks spoil the broth :: Many hands make light work

One swallow does not a summer make :: Where there's smoke, there's a fire

Source: Communicology: Joseph A. Devito.

Bibliography

Aitchison, Jim. 2007. *Cutting Edge Advertising*. Singapore: Pearson Education South Asia.

Baron, Naomi S. 2000. *Alphabet to Email*. London: Routledge.

Barron, Frank. 1969. *Creative Person and Creative Process*. New York: Holt, Reinhart & Winston.

Beg, Mirza Khalil, 1991. *Psycholinguistics and Languages Acquisition*. New Delhi: Bahri Publication.

Berners-Lee, Tim. 1999. *Weaving the Web*. London: Orion Business Books.

Brown, G., and G. Yule. 1983. *Discourse Analysis*. Cambridge: Cambridge University Press.

Chadda, Savita. *Nai Patrakareta Aur Lekhan*. New Delhi: Takshila Prakashan.

Chomsky, Noam. 1965. *Aspects of the Theory of Syntax*. Cambridge: MIT Press.

Chunawala, S.A. and Sethia, K.C.. 2001. *Foundations of Advertising Theory & Practice*. Mumbai: Himalaya Publishing House.

Cordon Jr., John C. 1975. *Semantics and Communication*. New York: Macmillan Publishing Co. Inc.

Crystal, David. 2000. *Language and the Internet*. Cambridge: Cambridge University Press.

Dev, Harsha. 2001. *Uttar Aadhunik Media Taknik.* New Delhi: Vani Prakashan.

Godre, Vinod. 2000. *Hindi Patrakarita: Swaroop evam Sandarbh.* New Delhi: Vani Prakashan.

Grosjean, Francois. 1982. *Life with Two Languages: An Introduction to Bilingualism.* Cambridge: Harvard University Press.

Gumperz, J. John. 1982. *Discourse Strategies.* Cambridge: Cambridge University Press.

Hall, Edward T. 1959. *The Silent Language.* New York: Doubleday.

Halliday, Michael. 1978. *Language as Social Semiotic.* London: Edward Arnold Ltd.

Harrison, Tony. 1987. *A Handbook of Advertising Technique.* London: Kogan Page Ltd.

Hatwal, A.K. *Vigyapan Kala.* Jaipur: Rajasthan Granth Akademi.

Hepner, H.W. 1961. *Advertising: Creative Communication with Consumers.* New York: McGraw Hill.

Hudson, R.A. 1980. *Sociolinguistics.* Cambridge: Cambridge University Press.

Inglis, Fred. 1972. *The Imagery of Power: A Critique of Advertising.* London: Heinemann Educational Books Ltd.

Jethwaney, Jaishri, and Shruti Jain. 2006. *Advertising Management.* New Delhi: Oxford University Press.

Leech, Geoffrey N. 1966. *English in Advertising.* London: Longman Green & Co. Ltd.

Levinson, Stephen C. 1983. *Pragmatics.* Cambridge: Cambridge University Press.

Leymore, Varda Langholz. 1975. *Hidden Myth: Structure and Symbolism in Advertising.* London: Heinemann Educational Books Ltd.

Malik, Lalita. 1994. *Sociolinguistics.* New Delhi: Anmol Publications Pvt. Ltd.

Marshall, Jim, and Angela Werndly. 2002. *The Language of Television.* London: Routledge.

Miller, George A. 1969. *The Psychology of Communication.* Baltimore: Penguin.

Morris, Charles. 1953. *Signs, Language and Behaviour*. New York: Prentice Hall.

Naughton, John. 1999. *A Brief History of the Future: The Origin of the Internet* London: Weidenfeld & Nicolson.

Nida, Eugene A. 1955. *Customs and Culture*. New York: Harper & Row.

Offeredi, Mariola. 1990. *Language versus Dialect*. New Delhi: Manohar.

Ogilvy, David. 1995. *Ogilvy on Advertising*. New York: Vintage Books.

Palmer, I.R. 1981. *Semantics*. Cambridge: Cambridge University Press.

Pandya, Indubala H. 1977. *English Language in Advertising*. Delhi: Ajanta Publication.

Potter, Simeone. 1975. *Language in the Modern World*. London: Andre Dentsch Ltd.

Reah, Daunta. 2002. *The Language of Newspapers*. London: Routledge.

Sandage, C.H., and V. Fryberger. *Advertising Theory and Practise*. Homewood: Richard D. Irwin Inc.

Scollon, Ron, and Suzie Scollon. 2003. *Discourse in Place: Language in the Material World*. London: Routledge, Taylor & Francis Group.

Sharma, Ram Avtar. 1995. *Abhivyanjana Shilpa aur Hindi Patrakarita*. New Delhi: Radha Publications

Stubbs, Michael. 1983. *Discourse Analysis*. Oxford: Blackwell.

Thakur, D. 1999. *Semantics*. Patna: Bharti Bhawan.

Thomas, Sunny. 1997. *Writing for the Media*. New Delhi: Vision Books Pvt. Ltd.

Tiwari, Sanjay. 2003. *The (Un)common Sense of Advertising: Getting the Basics Right*. New Delhi: Response Books.

Trudgill, P. 1980. *Sociolinguistics: An Introduction*. Harmondsworth: Penguin Books.

Turner, G.W. 1973. *Stylistics*. Harmondsworth: Penguin Books Ltd.

Valladares, June A. 2000. *The Craft of Copy Writing*. New Delhi: Response Books.

Verma, Shivendra K. 1993. *Aspects of English Language Teaching.* Chennai: TR Publications Pvt. Ltd.

Wells, William, John Burnett and Sandra Moriarty. 2003. *Advertising: Principles and Practice.* New Delhi: Pearson Education Inc.

Widdowson, J.D.A., and F.C. Stork. 1977. *Learning about Linguistics.* London: Hutchinson Educational Ltd.

Young, James Webb. 1960. *A Technique for Producing Ideas.* Chicago: Crain Communication.

Yule, George. 1995. *The Study of Language.* Cambridge: Cambridge University Press.

Journals & Periodicals

The following journals and periodicals have been of great help to me in crystallising my ideas.

1. *World Englishes:* Journal of English as an International and Intranational Language.
2. *Language:* Journal of Linguistics Society of India.
3. *System:* An International Journal of Educational Technology & Applied Linguistics.
4. *Language in Society:* Cambridge University Press.
5. *Language and Communication:* An Interdisciplinary Journal.
6. *Indian Linguistics:* Journal of the Linguistics Society of India.
7. *Journal of Linguistics:* Published for the Linguistics Association of Great Britain.

Besides these, various issues of *Brand Equity* (of *The Economic Times*), *India Today*, *The Brand Reporter* and *The Times of India* have helped me to develop a sound understanding of the Indian advertising scenario.

Index